THE ULTIMATE REAL ESTATE INVESTING BEGINNER'S BOOK

ACHIEVE FINANCIAL FREEDOM WITH RENTAL
PROPERTIES USING PROVEN FINANCING STRATEGIES
AND WEALTH-BUILDING TECHNIQUES

FRANK EBERSTADT

TABLE OF CONTENTS

Part III
PROFIT AND PROSPER

INTRODUCTION

When you think about real estate investing or simply purchasing a property, it can seem like something only rich people do. However, this is definitely not the case, and one man's story highlights this. Shaun Conlon was a pretty average guy from Ireland. He came from humble beginnings and decided to move to Chicago to earn some money. He started working as an assistant janitor, which didn't pay much. He painted apartments at night to make some more money and kept up with his routine for a few years. He saved up as much money as he could and bought an apartment after a few years. He then sold his apartment and made a profit, which was highly motivating for him. He got a taste of real estate investing and decided that this was what he wanted to do. He kept his job, but he invested in real estate and began selling real estate as a side job. He did this for over three years and became a top real estate broker. Then, he landed his first job at a brokerage and continued to hone his skills. About four years later, he was able to open his own real estate investment firm. He now uses real estate as his primary source of income, and it all started from a humble beginning.

"I was an ordinary person who did some fairly extraordinary things. It's America. You can still do those things."

— SEAN CONLON

The story simply highlights that anyone can get involved in real estate investing. It doesn't matter if you have tons of money to play with or just a few dollars in your piggy bank. There are strategies and ways in which you can dip your toes in the wonderful pool of real estate. Before moving on, it is important to understand what real estate investing is in the first place. When you invest in real estate, you are essentially investing in properties. You are using real estate as an investment vehicle to gain profit. There are many ways to generate a profit through real estate, and throughout this book, we will dive into each one of these methods and topics so you can fully understand how diverse real estate can be.

The two major categories of real estate are residential and commercial. Residential real estate is the type of property people live in, and commercial real estate is typically used to generate income on a larger scale. We are going to dive more into these two types of real estate, and many others, in the first chapter of this book. Real estate is multifaceted, and it's important to understand all the different types of real estate as well as all the ways you can invest. The reason anyone can invest in real estate is that there are so many options out there. You can tailor your investment strategy to suit your needs and goals.

Another common concern that people may have about investing in real estate is that it seems too risky. Property is expensive, and if you're putting a lot of money into something, you want to have a guaranteed positive outcome. I would love to say that you are guaranteed to make a lot of money through real estate, but we must realize that any kind of investing comes with its own level of risk. That being said, real estate tends to be one of the most stable forms of investment since property has a trend of increasing in value over time. Now, there are a few things that you have to consider, such as the location, amenities, and type of property, but this rule rings true if you do your research and choose the right property to invest in.

You don't have to be a homeowner first or choose the perfect time in the market to start investing in real estate. Your property investment journey can start right now, and it can be fruitful and rewarding. In fact, the longer you take, the more you delay the potential benefits of real estate investing. While there may be many excuses that you can make to not take the plunge into real estate investing, it simply means that you are delaying your potential wealth-building. Real estate is a cornerstone element for building your wealth, and it's a tool you can use to help reach your financial goals and additional stability in your life and future.

By the end of this book, you should have all the tools, tricks, and knowledge you need to confidently invest in real estate. The goal is to give you a comprehensive understanding of real estate investing as well as practical and actionable steps. This book is not just theory; there are also actions that you can take to help push you toward the right real estate investments. Interactive learning tools have been incorporated throughout the book to assist you with grasping concepts and give you practical aid along your real estate investment journey. All of this will help you have confidence in your decision-making so you can forge a path to financial freedom.

This book has been designed on a three-part framework. This way, you can first build a foundation and then work your way up into other aspects of real estate investing. The first part is going to be building the base. This essentially means that you will be building a firm foundation for your real estate knowledge. In this part, there are two chapters, and the overarching topics discussed will be the types of real estate investing and how to finance your real estate investments. Part two is about mastering the fundamentals and has three chapters within it. These three chapters cover the metrics of valuation, risk assessment, and actually purchasing your property. Finally, we have part three, which is about making a profit and prospering on your real estate journey. In this phase, there are five chapters, and the topics covered are tax benefits and legal considerations, passive income, short-term rentals, long-term success, and wealth building.

All of these parts are essential to investing successfully in real estate. They will give you all the knowledge you need to walk into your real estate investment journey with full confidence. By the end of this book, you should be well-equipped and ready to go. So many people wish they had started their real estate investment journey earlier in their lives. Regardless of your current life situation or your financial standing, you are in a good position to start investing in real estate. Simply picking up this book and taking the first step in the process already puts you on the right path. This is exactly where you need to be to find success when investing in real estate.

I have guided people through the process, and none has ever regretted it. Investing in real estate is one of the most fulfilling, exciting, and rewarding journeys you will ever go on. You don't have to make all the mistakes other people make because you now have the handbook and the directions away from all the pitfalls. I have already written books on Airbnb and how to use short-term rentals to build wealth. I have done it myself and, through these best-sellers, have guided others along the process. If you are interested, you can add to the knowledge from this book with guidance from my other books. This could be essential reading should you want to become an Airbnb host. Here are the titles:

- *How to Set Up and Run a Successful Airbnb Business:* Outearn Your Competition with Skyrocketing Rental Income and Leave Your 9 to 5 Job Even if You Are an Absolute Beginner
- *How to Unleash Your Airbnb's Full Potential:* The Complete Step-By-Step Guide to Maximizing Bookings, Rental Income, Setting Up Automation and Optimizations for Your Short-Term Rental Business

If you have ever wanted to invest in real estate but were unsure how to do it, you are in the right place. From here, we will build the base with Chapter 1 so you can fully understand the different types of real estate investing out there. Next, we are going to move on to two different topics that will build a robust framework for you to continue on your real estate investment journey. So, without further delay, let's jump into the first chapter.

PART I

BUILD A BASE

TYPES OF REAL ESTATE INVESTING

Ninety percent of all millionaires invest in some form of real estate (Red Oak, 2022). This is an incredibly high number and demonstrates that real estate is a viable option for building wealth and creating financial security. If nine out of ten millionaires choose to add real estate to their investment portfolio, then this is something that a beginner investor or somebody looking to build wealth should also look into. It is clear that real estate is a fantastically valuable asset in your overall investing portfolio.

An individual investor can invest in many types of real estate. This makes real estate investing even more attractive because you can find a type of real estate investment that is going to fit you and your goals perfectly. In order to make the right decision, it is important to understand the different types of real estate that you can invest in.

RESIDENTIAL REAL ESTATE

The first type of real estate we are going to be talking about is called residential real estate. This is one of the most popular types of real estate investments since it is accessible to the average person. On top of that, any person who has purchased a property, rented, or is in the housing market would have some experience with residential real estate, making it much easier to transition into this investment vehicle. Under the umbrella of residential real estate, you can purchase different kinds of properties, and each has its benefits and things to consider before investing.

Single-Family Homes

When it comes to residential properties, a single-family home is definitely one of the most popular and most common varieties out there. Not only are plenty of single-family homes currently on the market but there are also many constantly under development. This means there will be even more being brought onto the market. As the name implies, a single-family home is designed to meet the needs of a family. There are many varieties of properties that can fall under the category of a single-family home, and these include freestanding homes, cottages, villas, and even mansions.

These types of properties are incredibly popular with couples who have a family or are looking to establish a family. The reason for this is that there are key features in a single-family home that benefit the traditional family lifestyle. This includes having a garden, yard, or outdoor space for kids to play or adults to use for recreational and outdoor activities. These types of properties, specifically detached homes, also offer privacy because the home-owner would not be sharing space or walls with neighbors. The other benefit is that the homeowner has almost complete control over what they do with their property and can design and change things up as they see fit.

Multi-Family Homes

A multi-family home is more like an apartment or a duplex. With these types of properties, the people living within it will be sharing space and walls with their neighbors. From an investment stand-point, purchasing a multi-family home could be a good option because you can have multiple renters in one property, which means you are collecting multiple streams of rental income. Something that investors are doing with multi-family homes is called house hacking. This is when you stay in a portion of the property and then rent out the rest to a tenant. The tenant contributes to or covers the entire cost of the mortgage payment, which means you, as the investor, get to stay on the property for a fraction of the cost or completely for free.

Multi-family homes have a different target audience than single-family homes. Since there are communal living spaces such as gardens, lounges, and other areas, it may not be as attractive for larger families. These properties can be quite convenient to stay in, as many multi-family homes or apartments are close to city centers.

Condos

A condo or condominium is very similar to an apartment or a multifamily home, but these are typically situated in a larger building. Condos often offer more space than apartments and come with distinct ownership; each condo unit is individually owned, while apartments are usually rented. These types of properties have some shared amenities, but they do offer individuality, which means they are a blend of single-family and multi-family homes. There is a sense of community since many of the living spaces are shared, and you live in close proximity to your neighbors. On top of that, most condominiums are in desirable areas such as urban centers and cultural hubs, meaning the location is advantageous to many people, which can bring up the property's price.

Townhouses

With a townhouse, you are looking at a semi-standalone building attached to a collection of other houses or buildings. In many cases, a townhouse will offer a small yard, and you can think of a townhouse as a smaller version of a single-family home. There will be some shared amenities if the complex has a pool or communal gathering area. However, everything else is more private.

Sometimes, a townhouse will share a wall with a neighbor but offer the separation of a standalone house. These properties tend to be more affordable because they are smaller than single-family homes and are usually lower maintenance.

Mobile Homes

When considering investing in property, a mobile home may not be the first thing that comes to mind, but it is definitely an option. A mobile home is essentially a living space that is movable. To move these types of homes, you need to attach them to a specialized trailer or truck. It will have wheels so it is easily movable from place to place. It is also important to consider that a mobile home is designed differently, so you must understand the ins and outs of your particular mobile home to know how to move it and take care of it.

A mobile home is definitely more affordable than other real estate options, and it offers the flexibility of moving from place to place. These days, you can get some pretty advanced mobile homes with different rooms and living spaces that offer a lifestyle similar to that of a traditional home. There is also the option of permanently placing a mobile home on a support system that will act as a foundation. To do this, you need to rent or purchase the land on which you place the mobile home.

COMMERCIAL REAL ESTATE

The next category of real estate investment property is commercial real estate. For a property to fall under the category, it needs to generate profit through rental income or capital gains. It typically does not include properties that people live in from day to day.

Retail Spaces

The first category of commercial real estate is retail spaces. If you go to a shopping mall, you will see many stores, and the shop owners have to rent out these rooms or spaces in order to sell their products there. A restaurant or any other business that you might find in a shopping mall is also located in a retail space. There are also retail spaces that are a lot bigger and standalone. For example, if you visit a huge store like a Walmart or Costco, it may be a big center that stands alone without other stores around it. These still count as retail spaces.

Office Spaces

Offices are another option for commercial real estate buildings. This still generates income, even though there is no direct buying and selling of items from the office space. These spaces may be small suburban office buildings where only one company works or an office park where multiple companies rent the spaces. From an investor's point of view, these types of properties can be a lot more expensive to purchase, as an office building is quite a large investment but also generates a large amount of profit.

Industrial Properties

An industrial property is typically located outside an urban or suburban area. These types of properties are used for manufacturing, assembly, warehousing, and a mixture of all of these. These types of buildings need to be customized for the type of operations that will be running within them. Industrial property needs to be quite large because of the nature of the work occurring within the property. Some special licenses and permits may be needed for an industrial property due to the type of activity that is taking place.

Hotels and Motels

Even though people stay in hotels and motels, they are still categorized as commercial property. This is because they provide a service, and there may also be restaurants, boutiques, and shops within it. There are many different types of hotels and leisure properties out there. These could include ones that are full service, which means there is room service and a restaurant on site, whereas limited service means it is likely just going to provide the room for the guest to stay and may not have room service or a restaurant on site. There could also be extended stay rooms or options, such as an area equipped with a kitchen so guests can stay for longer periods. Resorts are also in this category, and they offer both full service and a large amount of land where people can take part in many recreational activities.

REAL ESTATE INVESTMENT TRUSTS (REITS)

A real estate investment trust is a great option for those who are looking to dip their toes into the water of real estate investment. The truth is that many forms of real estate investment come with a hefty price tag. It can take months or even years to save up enough to invest in real estate or build up your credit so that you can take out a loan to invest. A REIT helps you invest in real estate without having access to a large amount of funds. On top of that, you don't have to physically buy or manage property in order to invest.

The aim of a real estate investment trust is to create a liquid investment out of an illiquid asset. A REIT will combine the contributions from multiple investors to invest in property. Then, the profit from these investments will be shared among all who have contributed. REIT can invest in various kinds of properties, including complexes, townhouses, hotels, infrastructure, office buildings, shopping centers, warehouses, and residential real estate. This means an investor can diversify their real estate investment portfolio by simply investing in one thing. On top of that, investors do not have to put a lot of money into getting started with real estate investing. This makes real estate investing a lot more accessible and allows you to invest and get used to the real estate market as soon as possible. Since this type of investment is managed by somebody else, not all your money will be invested in real estate. Some of your money will be put toward a fee for the management of your investment.

There are three main types of REITs: equity, mortgage, and hybrid. Equity REITs are the most common and are equity-based, meaning that revenues are typically brought in through rent charged to tenants. Mortgage REITs will lend money to property owners through loans or invest in mortgage-backed securities.

Revenue is primarily generated from the interest earned on these loans and securities. Finally, hybrid REITs mix both of the above strategies into one portfolio.

DEVELOPMENT AND LAND INVESTING

Investing in land means purchasing the raw land that property can be built upon or used for other purposes to generate revenue. There are many types of land investing out there, so interested investors should understand what they want to do with it and what type of investment they are trying to make. Regardless of how you choose to use the land, if it's an investment, you must choose the right location. A terrible location will not have much value and will, therefore, be a poor investment.

Whether the location is good or bad depends on what you will use the land for. If you want to build a house on the land, then you need to choose a location that is convenient and close to everyday amenities that the average family would need. If you want to build a warehouse or some sort of commercial property, you need to ensure that the land you purchase is an ideal location. For example, if you are looking to use the land for commercial purposes, you need to ensure that it is easy to get to so that people can either shop, live, work, or participate in recreational activities there. Other uses for the land could be farming practices, such as raising livestock or growing crops.

It is also possible to purchase a piece of land and not do anything with it besides basic upkeep and then sell it for a higher price later on down the line. Land appreciates in value, so it will continue to increase in value, especially if it is in a good location. If you are planning to build on the property, then it's important to budget accordingly. Building a house or other type of real estate costs a lot of money, and it also means that you will need to get the right people on board to help develop that land. It can also take quite a long time because you will need approval and paperwork in order to get started. This is why purchasing land to start a development may not be the best option for a beginner investor or somebody who wants to see their returns as soon as possible. However, if done correctly, this can be one of the best ways to make a large return on your investment.

HOUSE FLIPPING

House flipping is getting more popular, and for good reason. The goal of flipping a house is to purchase a property, renovate it, and then sell it as quickly as possible for a higher price than you bought it for. When trying to make the most profit from this, many investors choose to purchase undervalued properties. The property may not have been taken care of, or there might be something wrong with it that has caused it to drop in value. The investor will purchase the property and make the necessary repairs to bring the property price back up. The newly refurbished property can be sold for more, and the investor makes a profit in a short amount of time.

When investing in this way, it is important to research and ensure you understand the property you are purchasing. If there is too much damage or the renovations are going to cost you a lot of money, then it's not going to be worth purchasing. Any renovation or additional cost needs to be less than the potential profit you could make from selling the house. The positives to taking part in this type of real estate investment are that you get to diversify your real estate investment portfolio and have an investment with a quick turnaround time. When it comes to real estate investments, few options offer you a quick turnaround time so that you can get your profit soon after investing.

While flipping a house could be a wonderful addition to your investment portfolio, you also have to take into consideration that it is a risk. The goal of flipping a house is to sell it quickly, but there are no guarantees. You will be taking a risk of some financial loss or having to hold the property for longer than you might expect. You will also need to do your due diligence in terms of research when it comes to the renovations, as you need to make sure that you have enough finances available for the renovation costs. It is always a good idea to plan to spend more money than you think you'll need, as there may be unexpected costs along the way. Planning is always key in any kind of real estate investment, and flipping is no exception.

BUY, REHAB, RENT, REFINANCE, REPEAT (BRRRR)

While this acronym might be funny to say, this is a very legitimate method in real estate investing. It follows a very similar principle to house flipping, as you will purchase a distressed property and then rehab it to make a profit. However, instead of selling the property, you will rent it out. From here, you will then refinance the property by taking a cash-out refinance. With this money, you will buy other properties that need to be refurbished and rented out. The great thing about this method is that you use little of your money to invest. You are using the money from the refinancing to purchase a new property, and since you are renting out your properties, you are constantly making an income.

The goal is to build on the momentum and continue to repeat the process so that you can build a robust real estate portfolio. There are definitely risks when it comes to this method, as investing in a distressed property may not always be as easy as we would like. There could be damages and issues with the property that you cannot see at first glance, so you must get a professional to inspect the property before you make a purchase. This way, you are completely aware of what needs to be done and whether it's going to be worth it for you to purchase the property. You should also consider any legal limitations that specific areas or properties might impose for certain types of renovations or changes. Having a legal professional on your team is really going to help you and save you a lot of time and money. However, if you can find a good property to get started, then you can continue building on this and bring in a satisfying amount of income through this investment method.

VACATION RENTAL PROPERTIES

With the rise of vacation rental websites, such as Airbnb, it has become a lot easier for people to market their vacation or short-term rentals to the public. This can make you a lot of money if you are willing to open up your property to tourists and travelers. When you rent out your property as a vacation rental, it is essentially private accommodation for a short-term stay. It differs from a hotel, and you can decide what kinds of amenities you offer to your guests. Since this is a short-term rental property, it needs to be fully furnished so that people can have a comfortable stay. On top of that, you will need to ensure that you are giving your guests an enjoyable experience because they can rate your property and the service they get on many of the vacation rental websites. You must maintain an excellent reputation because word-of-mouth is a great marketing technique, and you want people to talk positively to their friends and family so you can get more bookings.

When it comes to a vacation or short-term rental, knowing what you are offering is important. Location is also really important, as you need to have a property somewhere where people actually want to stay—for example, a cottage on the beach or an apartment in a big city. If you have a property close to any popular tourist destination, then you are already a suitable candidate to have a vacation rental. If you want to purchase a property as a short-term rental, then make sure you choose the right location and pick somewhere where people will travel and want to stay.

Since there are people in and out of your property, you can make more money than if you rented out the property on a long-term basis. You could have multiple tenants or guests within a month and make a huge profit. With this being said, it is important to consider that there will be periods when people are not as willing to vacation or travel. For example, during the summer months, vacation homes and vacation rentals will be more popular since more people are traveling. However, when it gets to the colder months or when work tends to pick up, such as the financial year-end, it may be a low season when people are not traveling as much. In these seasons, you may not make a lot of money.

Another thing that you need to consider is higher maintenance requirements when it comes to vacation rentals since multiple people use the space. It is also your responsibility to ensure that the space is safe. Short-term rentals also mean having to turn around the property for your new guests so it is clean and ready for their stay. This means it is not a completely passive form of income since you will need to actively check up on the property, ensure your guests are fine, and make sure that the property is up to scratch for each one of your guests when they check in. If there are complaints or emergencies from your guests, then you will need to rush to their side in order to assist them. If you do not have the time to take care of a short-term rental, you can hire a property management company to do it for you. This does come at a cost, but it may be worth it since you do not have to handle the day-to-day running of the property. This is also a good option if you have multiple rental properties you are trying to manage.

INTERACTIVE ELEMENT: WORKSHEET TO DETERMINE PERSONAL INVESTMENT PREFERENCES

Asking the right questions is essential when determining your investment goals and preferences. Go through this worksheet to help you understand your preferences and investment style. Remember to answer the questions honestly.

Scan the QR code to download a printable version of all interactive elements.

What is your primary goal when it comes to real estate investing?

_____

How much money do you aim to use as an initial investment?

_____

How comfortable are you with high-risk investments that can potentially lead to higher returns?

_____

Do you prefer:

1) A stable, lower-risk property with modest returns.

2) A higher-risk property with high earning potential.

_____

Would you prefer to hire a property manager or take a more do-it-yourself approach?

_____

List the properties discussed in this chapter in order of what interests you most to least.

_____

_____

_____

There are many types of real estate you can invest in, and this is a good thing. You get to choose the types that best suit your needs and speak to you the most. This is an important decision, so take some time to think about it. We discussed the different ways you can invest in real estate and the strategies you can use. As a beginner, choosing one to focus on is best; from there, you can grow your investment portfolio.

Now that you have a clearer picture of the various real estate investment options and have assessed your personal preferences, it's time to explore how to finance these investments.

FINANCING YOUR INVESTMENTS

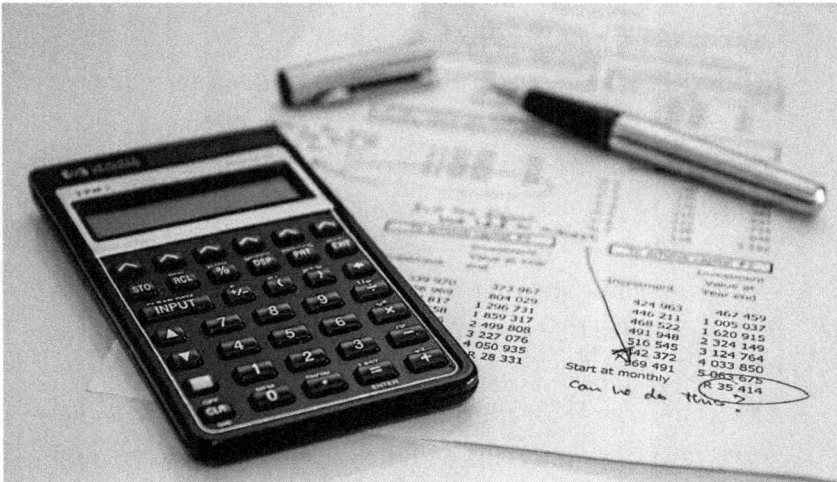

When it comes to investing in real estate, over 80 percent of buyers finance their investments (National Association of Realtors, 2018). This means that most people who own property or invest in real estate are not buying with cash but rather financing their investments. Financing means borrowing money from someone else, often a financial entity, in order to have the funds to make your investment. There are many ways to do this, so in this chapter, we will dive deeper into the topic.

FINANCING KEY TERMS

- **Interest Rate:** This is a percentage fee placed on a loan's principal amount.
- **Principal:** The amount borrowed without the addition of any interest.
- **Amortization:** A method of accounting used to distribute or spread loan payments over a specified period of time, in which each payment covers both principal and interest.
- **Loan-to-Value:** This is a ratio that is worked out by taking the loan amount and dividing it by the asset purchased or any collateral being borrowed against.
- **Lenders Mortgage Insurance:** A type of insurance that protects the lender. As the investor, you need to pay if you are borrowing over 80 percent of the value of the property you want to purchase.
- **Collateral:** A way to secure a loan is by pledging an asset, so if you default on the loan and cannot pay it back, the lender can take that asset to recuperate the money you owe them.
- **APR:** This stands for the annual percentage rate and is the yearly cost of a loan. This will include all charges, fees, and interest rates.

There are many different financing options available. This is a good thing because it means you'll be able to find an option that works best for you. Since every investor is different and has different strategies and a different amount of money, it is important to choose the financing option that is going to suit your needs the best.

Traditional Loans

The most common way to finance a property is through a traditional loan. There are a few different types of traditional loans, and you must consider the service provider. Each financial service provider will have their own terms and rules surrounding specific loans, so it is important to not only understand the type of loan you're taking out but also compare different service providers.

Fixed-Rate Mortgages

When the term fixed is used in financing, it means that there will be no change or movement. A fixed rate means there is a fixed interest rate for the entire duration of the loan. This interest rate is agreed upon prior to the loan being taken out, and it stays the same until you have paid off the loan in full or the loan term has ended. Many people choose this type of mortgage because the interest rate does not fluctuate with what is happening in the market. Since a mortgage or a home loan is a significant commitment that spans many years, having a fixed rate means more security and predictability.

Variable-Rate Mortgages

Conversely to a fixed-rate mortgage, a variable-rate mortgage has a monthly repayment that can change because the interest rate can change. This means it can either go up or down, and you pay either more or less. The benefit of this type of mortgage is that it allows you to overpay on your payments, which means you could potentially pay off your mortgage much more quickly. For example, if the rate moves to a lower percentage than what you usually pay, you could make your usual payment, meaning that you are paying over the required amount. This money is not lost but put toward your principal, helping you pay off your mortgage sooner.

The downside to this type of mortgage is that your payments will change over time. This will definitely affect how you budget and plan your future finances. You are also risking a higher interest rate than what you might have originally planned due to an uncertain economic situation. At the end of the day, the economic markets are unpredictable.

Interest-Only Loan/Mortgage

This type of mortgage is set up quite differently from the ones we have already discussed. With an interest-only mortgage, the borrower will only pay the interest required on the loan for a specified period of time. Once this time has elapsed, the borrower will owe the principal amount in a lump sum or based on an agreed-upon payment schedule. With other types of mortgages and home loans, you must repay the principal and the interest in your monthly repayments.

The benefit of this type of home loan is that you will pay back a minimal amount each month for the beginning portion of the mortgage term. This will help if you need some additional cash flow and expect your income to increase over the next few years. It may also be a good option for investors who are looking to flip the property or gain an income from the property in the coming years. This way, they are deferring larger payments to focus on their investments. However, it is a risk because you never know how finances are going to play out in the future, and once the interest-only portion of the mortgage term has ended, you will then be required to pay back the principal, and this means the overall monthly repayments are going to be much higher.

Balloon Mortgages

With a balloon mortgage, you will be required to make small payments for a certain period at the beginning of your loan term. This is followed by one large balloon payment once the term has ended. When taking out this type of mortgage, it is important to ensure that you will be able to afford the balloon payment at the end of the term. This type of mortgage can be tempting because the repayments are so low at the beginning. However, if you are not fully prepared to pay the balloon amount at the end of the mortgage term, it could result in you falling into a lot of debt, so ensuring that you have a plan in place is key if you are considering this type of mortgage.

Lease Options and Rent-to-Own

Let's first talk about a lease option, which is where you enter into an agreement with the current property owner to lease the property for a certain amount of time with the option to purchase it later down the line. This means that you have the opportunity to purchase the property once the lease is over. To have the chance to purchase the property, you, as the renter, will need to pay something called an "option fee upfront." This fee is included in your monthly rent and will also go toward the down payment of the property. This is not any kind of agreement to purchase the property, so the renter is not obligated to make the purchase after the lease has ended.

A rent-to-own agreement is exactly the same as a lease option but with a slightly different name. There is no obligation to purchase the house after the lease expires, but the current property owner can only sell after first giving you the option to purchase it as the renter. If the agreement is a lease-purchase contract, then you are required to purchase the property once the lease comes to an end.

This option is good for those who are trying to save up for a bigger down payment or simply do not have the funds to purchase the house outright and would like to rent first. Once the lease ends, the renter is required to purchase the property.

Seller Financing

With a traditional mortgage, you must go to a financial service provider and apply for the loan. The service provider will pay for your mortgage, and you will pay them back in monthly installments. An alternative to this financing method is called seller financing. With this method, the seller of the property will act as the mortgage lender. All this means is that there is no intermediary, and you will pay your mortgage installments directly to the person selling the property. This is a unique situation, and you will need to find a seller who is willing to enter into this kind of financing agreement. If you find somebody willing, you get to skip a lot of the red tape associated with getting a mortgage and can handle all transactions directly with the seller of the property. In this case, the seller will set out the mortgage and down payment terms. You may also be able to negotiate better if you are doing it directly with the seller of the property.

Cash-Out Financing

If you are looking for a way to access the equity that is currently sitting in your properties, then a cash-out refinance could be a good option for you. Essentially, when you apply for a cash-out financing option, you are replacing the mortgage you have at that moment with a larger loan, and the difference is given to you in a lump-sum payment. You can choose to use this money however you would like, but from an investment point of view, most investors will use it to invest in other properties or their current property to increase its value. The rules for this type of financing will vary based on where you are and the financial service provider you decide to go with, but in most cases, you will need at least 20 percent equity in your home. This means you would have needed to pay off at least 20 percent of what you owe on the property before considering a cash-out financing option. It is also a good idea to ensure that the interest rate you are getting on the new loan is not much more than what you are currently paying; otherwise, this could be a bad financial move. These types of loans should only be taken out if you have a plan in place and know what you're going to do with the money.

Home Equity Line of Credit (HELOCs)

With this financing option, you can cash in on the equity you currently have on your property through variable-rate financing. HELOC is a revolving line of credit that works similarly to a credit card. When you take out this line of credit, you do not have to use it if you do not need it. You are free to borrow the money you need and repay it as you use it or whenever you choose to pay it back. Most people will use this type of financing to make improvements to their homes or other aspects of their property investments. It basically just gives you access to additional funds so that you can spend it in other areas.

GETTING PREPARED FOR FINANCING

The process of receiving financing for your property investments doesn't start when you are ready to make the purchase. It starts as early as possible in your life because having a good financial standing is incredibly important. You can prepare yourself for big purchases from the time you start earning your own money and building up your credit score.

Improving Your Credit Score

Your credit score is extremely important when it comes to making any kind of big purchase and getting a loan from a financial institution. The bank or other financial service providers will look at your credit score to determine whether or not you are responsible with your money and if they can trust you with a big loan. It is a risk for financial service providers to give out big loans at good interest rates, which is why they look at the credit score to mitigate this risk. When you have a good credit score, it's a lot easier for you to get financing. You will get a good interest rate and terms on your loan so that you do not have to pay more than you need to. You also have more financing options, so you don't have to go with whichever provider offers you any kind of loan.

You can check your credit score on any of the major credit bureaus, and this is completely free. Depending on how well you have managed your credit over the past few years, you will either have a good or bad credit score. A good credit score is typically over 620; anything lower can be considered bad or moderate. The goal is to get your credit score as high as possible so you can give yourself the best opportunity for your mortgage. It is always best to start off on the right foot with building your credit score, but if you have a lower credit score, you can also work to build it up. The tips we will talk about in this section will help you build your credit score from scratch or increase a low credit score.

The first thing you need to do is have a look at all of your bills and make sure you know when they need to be paid each month. Missing bill payments or paying them late has a negative impact on your credit score. If you have any debit orders, you also need to make sure there is money in your account when your debit orders are taken to ensure you are not missing those payments. It's helpful to move all your payment dates to the same day or week so it's easy for you to remember to pay them.

The next thing you need to do is look at all your credit card balances to see how much you owe on your credit cards. Then, you will need to work on reducing these balances as much as possible. Owing too much money on a credit card negatively affects your credit score. You should only use about 20 to 30 percent of your available credit at any time. This is a safe area to be in, but lowering it as much as possible will help you stay out of debt. This leads to the next point—making sure your credit utilization is also low. Credit utilization is how much of your available credit you are actually using, and when you keep it low, it shows that you can manage having this credit available.

While you are working toward building up your credit score, you must not add any additional debt. Try not to get any more credit cards or any additional loans. Building your credit score takes small steps. Every month is going to compound, and you will have a good credit score sooner if you stick to the plan.

Down Payment Requirements

An important thing to consider when you are looking into taking out a mortgage or other financing option for an investment property is your down payment. Most types of financing will require you to have a down payment ready. On top of that, the larger the down payment you have available, the smaller the mortgage loan you will need for your investment. In general, it is better to have a larger down payment, especially if this is your first investment. Typically, there is a 15 percent required down payment for most types of property financing, but it is advisable to save 20 to 30 percent of the property price as a down payment.

There are also some other requirements you should aim to hit before you start applying for mortgages and home loans. For example, having a credit score above 680 is going to be in your favor. If you can get it higher than this, you will put yourself in an even better position. You also want to make sure that your debt-income ratio is lower than 50 percent. This means that you are making twice as much as you owe on your debts. This just gives security to lenders, showing that you have the finances available to pay off your debts.

If you haven't started saving toward an emergency fund, this is a good time to start because having about six months' worth of reserve finances is essential in life. This is going to help protect your finances if unexpected situations occur in your life. On top of that, having these reserve finances shows lenders you are financially responsible and have finances available should you not have access to your salary or if there's some other unexpected emergency that needs to be taken care of. All these aspects play important roles when getting a home loan, as well as being able to manage one when you have it.

Saving for Your Down Payment

There are a few things that you can do to help yourself when you are saving for a down payment. This will take some sacrifice, but it will definitely be worth it when you can afford the property you really want to invest in. The first step when saving toward anything is to budget and cut down on unnecessary expenses. Most of us do not really know how much we are spending until we write it down and create a budget, and when you do this, it'll be a lot easier for you to see where your money is going and where you need to cut back. A budget will help you plan your finances in every area of your life.

Saving is incredibly important. There is only so much you are going to be able to save since you need to use your money for your daily expenses. Looking for ways to increase your income is essential when you are saving toward bigger purchases or any kind of financial goal. This way, you can create more revenue for yourself to work with, and you can save quickly. When it comes to saving, it is also important that you make it a priority. You can do this by creating an automatic transfer from your main account into your savings account. This way, you don't even have to think about saving; it is just done for you.

When you are saving toward a goal, it is important that you track your savings and see how you are progressing toward it. This will allow you to pick up on any potential saving pitfalls to resolve the issue as quickly as possible and get yourself back on track. You will also be able to recognize whether you are on track for your saving goals, and if you are not, then you can make a plan to adjust your current spending habits to align more with your goals. This is an excellent way to ensure that you put yourself in the best position to save money and reach your financial goals.

INTERACTIVE ELEMENT: CALCULATE YOUR LOAN-TO-VALUE RATIO

Loan-to-value is an important calculation to figure out if an investment will be a good choice or not. You can use this simple formula to work it out:

LTV% = (Loan Amount / Asset Value) x 100

When calculating your LTV, aim for a lower ratio. Lenders typically view lower LTVs more favorably, as they signify reduced financial risk for them. A lower LTV often results in better financing options, including lower interest rates, especially when the ratio is at or below 80%. However, achieving a lower LTV may require a larger down payment on your part.

You can fill out this worksheet to compare different properties and determine which will be the best investments.

LTV%	Loan Amount	Asset Value
35%	$140,000	$400,000

Financing is one of the most important things to think about when it comes to real estate investing. Since property is such an expensive asset, choosing the right type of financing could save you a lot of money or end up costing you in the end. It is always best to start preparing yourself as early as possible. In fact, you can start now, even before you have an investment in mind. With a solid grasp of financing options, it's time to go deeper into evaluating real estate investments. Next is Part 2 of our framework: Master the Fundamentals.

PART II

MASTER THE
FUNDAMENTALS

UNDERSTANDING KEY METRICS

A lex became an accidental landlord very early on in his life. By the time he was twenty-five, both his parents had passed away, and they left him with a condo in California. He didn't really know much about property investment and actually thought about selling the condo quite a few times. However, he decided to keep it even though he didn't even live in California. He hired a property management company to handle the day-to-day business since he could not do it himself. It didn't make him that much profit, but it wasn't a liability at that stage either. You could say that he almost completely forgot about it, but it gave him a little insight into property management and what it entailed.

Over the next few years, he prioritized saving toward his retirement and building up a good portfolio for his future. However, these investments were not making as steady progress as he would've liked. This led him to think about other options. One day, he remembered his condo in California, and even though it wasn't making him a great profit, he recognized that property could be a wonderful investment. This is when he started doing more research. He figured out why his property wasn't making that much and decided to fix some of the issues—or at least not make the same mistakes with his next investment. For example, he knew California was a very expensive state and that the rent you could charge was really not worth it, based on the expenses needed to run a rental. With this information, he decided to invest in property in cheaper states, which would help him turn a bigger profit. He also looked at properties that would appreciate in value, which meant purchasing properties at a cheaper price so he could increase the value and make more profit. He also ensured the properties he was looking to invest in had lower operating costs so he could maximize his potential profits.

Having a strategy in place really helped him to aggressively start investing and grow his real estate portfolio. With the strategy in place, it took him about four years, and suddenly, he owned thirty-five rentals that were bringing in a massive income. This was helping him to save toward his retirement and other financial goals, ensuring he and his family had financial security for the future. While it took him a while to realize the value of real estate, once he did, he was able to put a plan in place that really helped him to increase investment opportunities and make real estate a viable investment choice.

CASH FLOW

When it comes to investments or running a business, it is important to have cash flow. Speaking of cash flow, you'll notice that people refer to it as positive cash flow or negative cash flow. When you have a positive cash flow, it means that you have cash left after you have spent money on all of your expenses. It basically means that you are turning a profit. However, if you have a negative cash flow, it means that your expenses are more than what you are making. When you have negative cash flow, it means you don't have any money to continue to grow the business. It is highly important to ensure that you do everything you can to maintain a positive cash flow, as this will result in you having money to put into your investments and continue to grow your overall investment portfolio.

It is very easy to work out cash flow, and it is one of the most important numbers when it comes to your investments. It's a simple way to see whether you are making a profit and whether you will be able to pay your bills when it comes to your properties. If you have a negative cash flow, it indicates that you may be overspending in certain areas or that the investment you made is not viable. In some cases, you have a negative cash flow for one month, and then the next few months have a positive cash flow. Therefore, it is important to track your cash flow over the course of a few months so you can get a better idea of how your investments are performing.

When you have multiple properties in your real estate investment portfolio, it becomes even more important for you to track your cash flow. You will need the cash for the individual properties as well as the overall cash flow in your entire investment portfolio. Your overall cash flow will give you a snapshot of how your portfolio is performing, and cash flow for individual property investments shows you which ones are turning the most profit and which ones you will need to reevaluate. Cash flow is also an indicator of where you need to put in more work or effort to increase the profit of certain properties.

PROPERTY APPRECIATION

Property appreciation takes place when the value of a piece of real estate gradually increases over time. There are many reasons for the value increase, including the general real estate market, the economy, and improvements or renovations to the actual property. Appreciation is one of the fundamental ways many real estate investors make an income through their real estate investments. When investing in a property, the goal is to choose one with the best chance of appreciation.

In order to figure out whether a property is a good candidate for overall appreciation, you will need to look at a few key points. These are the market demand, economic indicators, and location. Market demand simply means that more people want to live in a certain area or purchase the property that you have. If there are more people who want to purchase properties in the area that you have invested in, the overall property prices will increase. You can gauge future market demand by looking at areas currently being developed and where other investors are choosing to put their money. As a first-time investor, you can also look at places that already have a high market demand to see if you can purchase any properties within or close to that area.

Economic indicators have a tremendous impact on all types of investments, and real estate is no exception. These economic indicators could be job growth or creation, interest rates, and inflation. If the economy is moving in a positive direction, the price of real estate will probably increase. However, in the case of an economic downturn, the price of property might decrease. It is important to understand that there are always highs and lows when it comes to the economy, so it will never be completely stable throughout the lifespan of your investments. However, you may be able to use it to your advantage if you do your research.

You could purchase properties when they are at a lower price, and then when the economy picks up again, these properties will appreciate in value and give you a larger profit.

Location is easily one of the most important aspects to consider when investing in property. People will pay a lot more money for a lot less if the location is good. We know this because properties in central hubs and big cities tend to be much more expensive to buy and rent than those on the outskirts or in inconvenient areas. You will probably pay double or triple the amount to buy an apartment in New York or London compared to what you would pay if you purchased a property of the same size in an outlying area. Location is so important because people want to live near employment opportunities, amenities, and safe neighborhoods and areas. This doesn't mean that you have to purchase properties in big cities, but you have to make sure that you are choosing the right location and that it is going to be somewhere where people want to live. Look for up-and-coming areas with good schools that are walkable, safe, and have all the necessary amenities nearby.

EQUITY

When we speak about equity, it simply represents how much of the property you actually own. It shows you how much money you would get from the property if you were to sell it immediately. To figure out your equity, you need to subtract the outstanding balance of your mortgage from the current market value of the property. If you sold the property immediately, you would need to pay off the mortgage before you could take any profit from it. This is why many investors do their best to pay off the mortgage as quickly as possible so they have more equity in their investments.

You can use or leverage equity in a way that is beneficial to your investments and overall profit. One way you can do this is by improving your property to increase the market value. Since the mortgage payments are already agreed upon and will not change, making improvements to the property to increase its value will not impact how much you owe on your mortgage but will impact how much the property is worth. When you sell the property, you will get a larger profit since the property is more valuable. You can make many types of home improvements, like adding new rooms and amenities and making the home more aesthetically pleasing.

You can also consider taking out a home equity loan, which allows you to get cash based on the equity of your current property. You will use that money to improve your current property or even invest in additional properties to continue growing your real estate investment portfolio. This needs to be done with caution, and you will need to ensure you do your research before taking out this type of loan. However, investments can increase your overall profit and make your investment portfolio more valuable.

NET OPERATING INCOME (NOI)

The net operating income is the income generated from operating your property after deducting operating expenses. This amount does not include your mortgage payments. However, it does include most other things that you will pay for when it comes to your property. This will include insurance, property management fees, maintenance, and property taxes. To figure it out, all you have to do is look at the total revenue your property is bringing in and measure it up to the total operating expenses. This is an important figure, especially if you are using your property to bring in some sort of income, for example, if you are renting out your property. However, if you are living in your property and not using it for any kind of current profit, then you do not need to work out NOI.

You never want to spend more money than you are making. If the net operating income is very low or is a negative amount, this is a good indication that you are either spending too much or charging too little. With this information, you will then change your strategy to either lower your expenses or increase the rent you are charging so you can make a good profit from your property. Remember that your total income is being considered when you are working this out, so ensure you include rental income and other sources of revenue that your properties are bringing in. This could be revenue from the use of amenities such as laundry machines or parking fees. You will then subtract the total expenses from your total revenue in order to get your net operating income.

CAP RATE

The cap rate, or capitalization rate, is the net operating income divided by the purchase price or current market value. This figure is calculated to help an investor measure the return on investment of a property. A cap rate helps investors estimate the return they may expect to generate on their investment property. It is important to recognize that this is not a set-in-stone number, and many things can affect a cap rate. This is simply a prediction or estimate that an investor can use when making decisions.

Many factors can affect a cap rate. These include location, the size of the property, market stability, growth potential, and capital liquidity. Many investors use a cap rate to compare potential investments and see which one will be the most profitable. They will take into account all the factors above and figure out which one of the potential property investments will be the most profitable for them. For example, imagine there are two properties that an investor has their eye on. They are very similar in every way, except they are in different geographical locations. The investor will need to take this into consideration. The geographical location affects the net operating income and the potential returns the property can make. One property could be in a remote location. That means profit will be lower. Operating expenses will also be lower. The property could be in a big city, but this means that the operating expenses will be more expensive, and the rent you can charge and the amount of money you can make through this property will be a lot more. From here, the investor can work out the cap rate to see which one is going to be more profitable and then decide which property to invest in. You can work out the cap rate with this formula.

Cap Rate = Net Operating Income / Current Market Value

INTERACTIVE ELEMENT: CALCULATE THE NOI FOR A SAMPLE PROPERTY

The best way to understand NOI is to do it yourself. This is easier than you may think. The first thing you need to do is work out how much your potential property will make. This includes rent and other income sources such as:

- Parking fees
- Cleaning fees—charges collected from guests or tenants for cleaning services
- Charges for amenities
- Vending machines
- Laundry

Next, you will need to determine how much the property's expenses will come to. Many expenses could come up; the most common are:

- Utilities
- Taxes
- Repair and maintenance
- Insurance
- Accounting fees
- Legal fees
- Property management fees
- Cleaning fees—costs paid by the landlord for cleaning services
- Marketing expenses

The next figure you will need is the Gross Operating Income. It can be worked out with this formula:

Gross Operating Income = Potential Rental Income – Vacancy Losses

After you have all three figures, you can plug them into this formula to find out the NOI of a property:

NOI = (Gross Operating Income + Other Income) – Operating Expenses

To practice this, you can choose a few properties currently listed for sale on a property website. Try to find out as much information about them as possible and follow the above steps to find out their NOIs. You can then compare to see the difference. You can use the template below.

Income

Name	Amount
Total	

Expenses

Name	Amount

Total	

After financial metrics, we now delve into property valuation and risk assessment. The next chapter helps you with these so you can make well-informed investment decisions.

4

PROPERTY VALUATION AND RISK ASSESSMENT

Camila decided she was ready to start on her real estate investment journey. She found a wonderful apartment that she believed she could rent out to bring in a significant income. The process was going smoothly, and she decided to make an offer on the property. While waiting for the final paperwork and the details to be finalized, she decided she wanted to get the property valuated by her property evaluation expert. Before this, she had simply trusted the seller on the value of the property. After a few days, her property evaluator came back to her and said that the property was valued at much less than she thought and much less than the offer she had put in.

She was quite surprised by this and went back to the seller to ask for clarification. The property owner was adamant that the original pricing was correct and that Camila's evaluator was the one who was wrong. Since Camilla had already made an offer, the property seller knew how much money was on the table and refused to bring down the price. After a few days of back-and-forth, Camilla was forced to let go of the property. This was a hard one for her because she really believed that this property would be the perfect investment. It took her six months to find another similar property that could offer her great investment benefits.

A lot goes into investing in real estate, and property valuation is one of the most important aspects. It's easy to look at a property and think it is valued at a certain amount, but once the property has been inspected, it could be a completely different result. Getting a property inspected will help to ensure that you are paying a fair amount for the property, and if you already own it, you will get a fair amount if you choose to sell it.

VALUATING PROPERTIES

Property valuation is simply the assessment that your property will undergo in order to determine its value based on various factors, including location, amenities, and size. Property valuation is an incredibly important step in any real estate process, not only for the people who are buying and selling but also for other aspects, such as property insurance and taxation.

During the property assessment, the property surveyor or inspector will look at all the space on the property. They will consider the condition, size, number of rooms, age, and any potential for future development of the property. It is highly important to get a reputable professional to do this so you can get an accurate property assessment. It is also a good idea to have your own property assessor look at a property that you are planning to buy. This will give you peace of mind and ensure you are not overpaying for a piece of real estate.

Home value can be broken up into three different categories. These are assessed value, fair market value, and appraised value. A tax assessor in your municipality determines the assessed value and is only used for tax purposes. If the value is high, then taxes will be high. Fair market value is the amount you would be expected to get if you sell your property. The appraised value is the price given to you after a professional appraisal has been done on the property and is a more accurate representation of the property's value and what the seller should expect to get for it.

CMA

CMA stands for comparative market analysis, and it is used to estimate a property's price based on similar properties recently sold in the same area. Real estate agents do this type of analysis and then give it to people who want to sell their properties so they're able to list at an appropriate price. Property buyers can also use this to make a competitive offer on a property they are interested in purchasing. While real estate agents use their own special tools to do this kind of analysis, you can also do a basic form of a CMA on your own. All you have to do is go onto property listing websites and see how much properties are going for, and this will give you a good idea of what you should expect to pay for a similar property or what you can expect other people to pay for a property that you are looking to sell.

You can expect a CMA report to include aspects such as location, size, square footage, age of the property, number of rooms and bedrooms, any special features, the date of the sale, and the terms of financing for the sale. If you're looking to do your own CMA, there are a few steps you'll need to go through to ensure it's as accurate as possible. First, you will need to have a look at the neighborhood and whether it is a pleasant neighborhood. A good neighborhood is typically identified through the amenities, cleanliness, safety, and proximity to transportation and other necessities.

Next, you have to look at the property and gather the relevant details. If you're looking to purchase a property, you can look at the online listing to get a general idea of what the property provides, but it is always best to do an in-person visit to ensure the listing details are accurate. When you do a visit, make sure that you look at the size of the home, style, age, condition, layout, and general livability of the space. You will then need to list three to five comparable properties in the same area. These properties should have been recently sold so you can get the closest comparison possible, as the price of real estate fluctuates quite quickly.

Once you have done this, you will need to adjust for any differences between the comparable properties you have used and the ones that you are interested in buying. Every property is going to have differences of some sort, so it is important to understand these and their monetary impact. Professionals have prices and values assigned to certain differences. For example, if the property you are looking to purchase has an extra bedroom compared to comparable properties, this will significantly impact the price, as an extra bedroom or bathroom adds value to a property.

CMAs are definitely not perfect, but they can give you a great idea of how much you should expect to pay if you purchase a property and how much you should expect to get if you were to sell your property. It allows you to plan and budget effectively before you make an offer or even start the purchasing process, ensuring you are not getting a bad deal when buying or selling your property. The CMA is essentially a base around which you can build your real estate investment pricing.

RISK ASSESSMENT

When it comes to investing in real estate, there will always be some risk involved. Typically, the more risk an investor is willing to endure, the higher the potential reward could come from the investment. With that being said, it is unwise to take risks without assessing the risk and seeing if the potential reward is actually going to be worth it. When we talk about risk, we're talking about losing the money that we have invested. When it comes to real estate, risk is more of a complicated topic because so many factors can play into a property's value. On top of the value, you also have to consider whether it would be easy to sell the property when the time comes or to rent it out to tenants.

When thinking about risk and how it affects real estate, there are several aspects to consider. The first aspect is the real estate market. We already know that this market is incredibly unpredictable, and while there are forecasts used for market prediction, in many cases, these are not completely accurate. When it comes to the market, things like supply, demand, government policies, and unforeseen national events can all play a huge part in the value of a property. It is a good idea to have a look at the market and see what the forecast is saying so that you can plan. Still, it is also important to recognize that unpredictability is the only thing that is predictable in the real estate market. With that being said, typically, the real estate market goes up over time, so even though there are pockets of time where the market will be in a downturn, it is highly likely that it will pick up again.

Structural risk is an important type of risk that must be considered when purchasing a property. Every property will have its flaws, but it is important to understand what these flaws are to make sure you are investing in something that will last for the long term and will not cost you a bundle to rectify. For example, something like a damaged foundation or mold within the building is going to cost you a lot of money to repair, and in some cases, it might be irreparable. However, smaller structural issues could be fixed and dealt with. Purchasing a property with some structural issues will probably be cheaper, but you have to consider the amount you will be paying to complete the repairs.

Location is easily one of the most important factors you need to consider when investing in any kind of real estate. With that being said, location can also be a risk factor, especially if the area is not good or goes downhill from the time that you purchased the property. It is highly important that you research the location before you make a purchase, as this will be one of the biggest factors to impact the value of your property.

Another risk factor to consider is liquidity and cash flow. When it comes to real estate, there is not a lot of liquidity available since all of your money is going to be tied up in the physical property. You

won't be able to quickly pull out some money from your investment for an emergency or if you want to purchase something else.
There is a long process to get your money out of a real estate
investment, so it is important to understand that even though
property increases your overall net worth, you might not have
access to that money until much later on. Cash flow is another
thing to consider, as a negative cash flow is an enormous risk to
any investor. Ensuring you make the right investments and set
yourself up for positive cash flow is essential. If you realize you are
going through a period where you have a negative cash flow, it is
important to figure out why this is so you can solve the problem
before you lose too much money.

A huge factor when it comes to real estate investment is your
tenants. If you rent out your property to other people, there will
always be a risk that they will not pay or they will not take good
care of the property. You can't control other people and what they
do, but you can ensure you do your research beforehand and don't
accept tenants simply because they have applied. There needs to
be a screening process before you allow somebody to move into
your property to ensure they will pay on time and take care of
your property. If they don't, you will spend a lot of time, money,
and effort trying to get your rent and fix any of the issues they
may cause. In line with this, another risk is vacancies if you
cannot find tenants for your property. If you have vacancies for
long periods of time, it means that you are not making money,
and your cash flow will go into the negative. There are many
things that could cause vacancies, such as the economic market or
the location of the property. In order to mitigate this, you will
need to ensure that you have done your research to purchase a
property that is in demand and that people will more likely want
to stay in. You will also need to price your property competitively
to attract more potential tenants. Marketing is also very impor-

tant, and it may be worth it to get a real estate expert on board to assist you.

We always talk about how property tends to appreciate in value over time, but another risk is property depreciation. If the property loses value over time, it is depreciating in value. It is important to choose the property you are going to invest in very carefully. Researching real estate markets and statistics when it comes to the type of property and its location will help you ensure you are setting yourself up for success with your investment. It is also a good idea to monitor the market even when you already have a property you have invested in. If you notice a risk of depreciation, it may be worth it to consider selling to save yourself from losing a lot of money. When it comes to investing in real estate, it is not simply purchasing a property and leaving it there. You will need to constantly be doing market analysis to ensure that you mitigate any risks as early as possible.

INTERACTIVE ELEMENT: CALCULATE THE CAP RATE OF A PROPERTY

In order to get the CAP rate of a property, you will first need to have the NOI. In the previous chapter, you worked this out for a sample property. You can use those figures in this exercise as well. Here is the formula for the CAP rate:

Cap Rate = Net Operating Income / Property's Sale Price or Market Value

There is a lot that can go into defining what a good cap rate is. Typically, between 8 percent and 12 percent is good, but in some cases, lower than this is also favorable.

After valuation and risk assessment, you're now ready to move forward with purchasing a property.

5

PURCHASING THE PROPERTY

An interesting statistic is that 75 percent of recent homebuyers have regrets about their purchase (Zillow, 2022). This is a huge number, and it can make people wonder whether real estate is actually worth it if so many people regret it. The reason so many new homeowners tend to regret their purchase is that the property requires a lot more maintenance and work than they initially expected. Knowing this, it's clear that many people who purchase property do not do the research they need to. It is so important to do the relevant research before you make such a big purchase. This regret can definitely be avoided if people knew what they were getting into and were prepared for it from the start.

PREPARING TO BUY

Preparation is key when you are looking to make a large purchase, like when it comes to real estate. You definitely don't want to be part of the 75 percent of people who have regrets about their purchase. There are many steps to take when it comes to investing in a property. Ensure that you are going through the steps and taking your time to ensure you are making the right investment for you and your needs.

Make Sure You're Ready

The first rule of buying a property is to make sure that you are actually ready to do so. This means being financially and emotionally ready because buying a property is a huge commitment. You will also need to consider whether buying a property right now will fit into your goals for the future. Consider how buying this property is going to affect your finances and your life for the foreseeable future. You may even want to list out a few pros and cons to get a balanced idea of where you are when making this huge investment.

Get Your Finances in Order

As you already know, purchasing a property is a huge financial commitment. In fact, it is one of the biggest financial decisions you can make. You'll have to take some time to look at your finances to see whether you can afford a property right now. Have a look at your current finances, including your income, debts, assets, and liabilities. Consider whether you could afford a down payment on the property and the subsequent monthly mortgage payments.

After you have looked at your finances, you may conclude that you cannot afford a property right now. That's completely fine, and it's much better to be honest with yourself from the beginning. The next step from here is planning your finances so that you will be able to purchase a property in the future. This may mean cutting down on your expenses so that you can save toward a down payment. It may also mean that you should be looking for ways to increase your income so that managing the mortgage payments will be easier for you. Understanding your finances will help you plan for your future real estate investments.

The Down Payment

Once you know how much you can afford or whether you can afford a property at all, it is time to save for your down payment. It is advisable to save about 20 percent of the price of the property as a down payment. The reason is that a larger down payment will decrease your monthly mortgage payment and make it easier for you to pay off the mortgage quickly.

With that being said, you do not need to put down 20 percent. Many people choose to put down a smaller down payment and then increase their monthly mortgage payments in order to pay off the mortgage quickly. Whatever you decide, it is important to have some money saved for your down payment before you start aggressively looking for properties. Once you have the down payment, the purchasing process is going to happen a lot more quickly because you can put in an offer and then make the payments almost immediately. If you are looking for property now and don't have the money for a down payment, it may mean that all of this is wasted effort because you cannot put in an offer or get a mortgage.

Find the Right Mortgage

Many types of mortgages and home loans are offered by a variety of financial service providers. When you are looking for a mortgage, you must take the time to compare quotes from as many financial service providers as possible. You should also look at the different types of mortgages to see which one suits your needs the best. Applying for the right type of mortgage will significantly increase your chances of getting the mortgage and make the entire process easier for you.

Start Preapprovals

Once you have decided which mortgage and which mortgage lender you want to go for, you can start the preapproval process. Apply for mortgages with various lenders at the same time. This is an excellent strategy because even if you get denied by one lender, you still have others who could approve your mortgage. Just make sure that you are happy with all the financial service providers and types of mortgages you are applying for. You will need to gather financial paperwork and fill out multiple forms to start the preapproval process. However, it is a lot easier to do everything in bulk because once you have sent the documents to one lender, you can simply use the same financial documents for all the others.

Get a Real Estate Agent

Having a real estate agent on board is going to make the entire process of looking for the right property much easier. You can look on your own, but you will not have access to all the connections and options that a real estate agent does. On top of that, real estate agents can be a really important asset when it's your first time investing in a property, as they can guide you through things that you may not have thought of.

You don't have to go with the first agent you meet with. You can interview a few real estate agents and see which one suits your needs the best. Asking your friends and family members which real estate agents they have used is a great way to figure out which agents are reputable and professional. You always want an agent who will be on your side and will help negotiate on your behalf.

Go Shopping

Now starts the fun part of the process. You get to look for your property. Your real estate agent will guide you to different sites and send you properties that match your needs and budget. Have a look at a variety of property listing websites and just start scrolling through until you find properties that suit your needs. Once you have decided on a few different properties, you can actually visit and do walk-throughs of your ideal properties. When you visit the properties, take some photos and write a list of pros and cons so that you can keep track of which properties you like the most and why. If the market is hot and there are many people looking for real estate in that area, you may not have a lot of time to make your decision. This is why it is important to keep track of your thoughts so that you know exactly whether this property is for you if you need to put in an offer quickly.

Make an Offer

Once you have found the property of your dreams, it is time to make an offer. This is when you tell the current owner of the property that you want to make a purchase and then let them know how much you're willing to pay. You can go back to your real estate agent and ask how much they are expecting and how much you should be offering. Once you put in the offer, it is the seller's turn to accept or reject it. If they reject the offer, you have the opportunity to make a counteroffer that might be more appealing to them. This may start discussions between you and them until you can find an offer that both parties are happy with. Sometimes, the seller will not accept your offer; in that case, you have to move on and find another property to invest in.

Get a Mortgage

If the offer is accepted, then you move on to getting a mortgage. At this stage, you should already have preapprovals, so you can choose a lender who has preapproved you. This process involves a lot of paperwork, so it is a good idea to ask your real estate agent what is required in your area for a mortgage. This way, you can get everything collected, so when you apply for the mortgage, it is a much easier process. Some documents that you need are your W-2 forms, pay slips for the last two months, proof of income, tax certificates, bank statements, details on any loans, and your personal details, such as your ID and Social Security number.

Get Homeowner's Insurance

In some cases, mortgage lenders will not give you a loan unless you have homeowner's insurance. Even if the mortgage lender does not state this is a requirement, getting homeowner's insurance is a good idea to protect you and your investment. The policy should only become effective on the closing date or the date of sale. The insurer will help you along in this process.

Home Inspection

Before the deal is closed, it is important to do a home inspection to make sure you know exactly what you're getting into. Even if you have visited the property, you could have missed underlying problems that could end up costing you a lot of money once the house is in your possession. Getting a professional to do the home inspection is the best way to go. If you find anything that was not disclosed in the initial stage, then you can bring it to the seller's attention, and you might be able to negotiate a lower price, or you might decide that you no longer want to purchase the property. Regardless of the outcome, it is definitely better to know what you're getting into before you proceed with the purchase.

Have the Home Appraised

Home appraisal is different from the inspection that was done in the previous step. When you get your home appraised, you are figuring out how much it is worth. Typically, your mortgage lender will organize the appraisal even though you will be paying for it. The lender will need to know exactly how much the house is worth before they give you the mortgage.

Negotiate Any Repairs

You are now nearing the end of the process, so it is time to negotiate. This can be done face-to-face or through your real estate agents. If there are any repairs needed, you can start negotiating these with the property seller. Remember to be realistic, as the outcome of the negotiations will depend on the kind of market you are currently in.

Close the Deal

Once you're happy with everything, it is time to close the deal. This means that you and the seller have now agreed on the terms of the sale, and your mortgage has been approved. Some closing documents will need to be filled out. At this stage, you will probably be asked to do a final walk-through of the property. This is to make sure everything is as it should be. Once all that is done, you can close the deal, and you are now a property owner.

QUESTIONS TO ASK BEFORE BUYING

You are going to be putting down a lot of money when you purchase your property, so it is important that you ask the right questions. You are free to ask any questions you would like when negotiating or deciding whether you want to purchase a property. It is far better to ask more questions than fewer questions. Here are a few that you should consider before you make an offer or make a purchase:

- How old is the house?
- When were the major appliances installed?
- How long until these appliances need maintenance or replacement?

- Were any major renovations done, and if so, when?
- Do you have any paperwork on the house's repairs, appliances, and systems?
- Are there any water-related or electrical issues with the house?
- Has the property been bought or sold multiple times? If so, what were the reasons for this?
- Are there any negative aspects or history with this property?
- Is there anything else that I would need to know?

THE UNDERWRITING PROCESS

Underwriting is a very important part of the process when it comes to purchasing a property. This is not done by you but by the financial service provider. The process involves evaluating and assessing any financial and risk-related aspects of the investment. Essentially, the financial service provider is doing the due diligence to determine whether or not it is feasible to invest or lend you money. If you are a professional real estate investor, then you will probably have some underwriters on your team who do this for you to make sure the investments are viable and good options for your goals.

When the underwriting process is underway, a few different things are done. One of the first things is a financial analysis, in which all the financial aspects of the investment are looked into. This will include the potential for income, expenses, cash flow, and other financial aspects that need analysis. At the end of the day, when you are a property investor, you want to make sure that your property is going to bring in an income.

Risk assessment and cash flow analysis are also done during this process to make sure that no unnecessary risk is being taken and that the property will be in a good position to have a positive cash flow. Market analysis will also need to be done to consider the effect the current real estate market may have on the income potential and the general viability of a property investment. Finally, the underwriting process needs to do its due diligence to gather and verify relevant information regarding the property. This is just to ensure all the information and reports are accurate so that potential issues are dealt with as soon as possible.

As a real estate investor, you can use techniques from underwriting in order to analyze and evaluate your potential real estate investment deals. The basics of underwriting are to assess risk and ensure that your investments will be viable in the future. You can conduct your own underwriting analysis since you will have access to the majority of the data and information needed. You can also get a third party involved to assist you with the underwriting process. This can be done by a financial advisor or a broker who will identify any blind spots or issues that you may have missed when you did your own financial and risk analysis. The underwriting process is important because it allows you to plan your future and mitigate risk when investing in property. Investing in property is definitely exciting, but it is important not to get carried away with the process. If there are any red flags, you should definitely take a step back and think about whether it is worth it. Property investors will tell you that there are deals that you simply have to walk away from after you have done the necessary analysis. It is far better to walk out on a potentially risky deal than be stuck in a situation where you are hemorrhaging money unnecessarily.

Underwriting is part of the process in which you prepare to buy a property. Many of the steps we discussed in the first section of this chapter apply to underwriting. For example, you will need to gather all of your information and documentation, fill out the necessary forms, be responsive and available to your underwriters throughout the process, and ensure that any financial activities you participate in are relevant to purchasing this property. When you're going through the process of purchasing a property, it is important to be very cautious about what you are doing in the financial space, as opening any new lines of credit or taking out a loan could be a complication in the assessment that will be done. You don't want anything to impede the underwriting process or the property purchasing process.

DUE DILIGENCE

This is the time between your offer for the property being accepted and the closing of the deal. At this stage, it is important to ensure you review all the aspects of the deal and the transaction before you close. This stage is put in place to ensure that you are happy with the deal and that there are no red flags that you might have missed through the other steps of the process. If you find something that doesn't sit well with you, or there has been miscommunication or outright deception regarding the property, then you are free to cancel the deal. Just because the offer has been accepted does not mean that it has been finalized.

After the offer has been made, the true process of due diligence really starts. The first thing that happens is a home inspection. This is a more formal home visit than the one that you might've done before you made the offer. You will get a property inspector to come in and identify any issues with the property. If any major issues have been found, then you can back out, or you can negotiate with the seller of the property to bring the price down or have them resolve the issues before you move in.

Next comes a home appraisal, which will evaluate the property's market value based on various factors. Once this is done, a title check will need to be conducted. This is done to ensure there aren't any lawsuits or claims on the property that either you or the current owner are not aware of or have not disclosed. This is done to protect you from any potential legal expenses you may not be prepared for down the road. The next step in the process is a land or property survey. This is done in order to map out and locate features, boundaries, improvements, and corners of the land your property is on. The goal of this survey is to show you exactly where your property ends and another property begins. In many areas, this survey may already exist and can be passed on from seller to buyer.

Enlisting the service of a real estate attorney is necessary to review all contracts and legal documents related to the purchase. This is a complicated process, and you don't want to miss something or make a mistake that could cost you down the line. The lawyer takes care of things like examining the purchase agreement, disclosure statements, and any documents from the homeowners association (HOA) or zoning regulations. A real estate attorney is someone on your side to give you valuable insight into potential legal issues and ensure that your interests are always protected.

Another important part of the process is disclosures, in which the seller needs to disclose all information about the property in a written document. What they disclose will depend on the laws in the local area and those on a federal and state level. You can talk with your real estate agent or legal advisor about what exactly the seller needs to disclose to you. Certain things will always need to be disclosed, regardless of where you live, including any health and safety risks and the presence of potentially dangerous substances like asbestos and lead paint.

Every area will have its own rules, dependent on the neighborhood or area. This is where a homeowners association comes in. Not all properties are covered by a homeowners association, but if the one you are considering is, you'll need to know what they expect and any bylaws or covenants that you will be bound to if you decide to purchase that property. Some HOAs have restrictions on renting out your property, decorations, and even design choices, such as the color of your house paint. There are also fees attached to HOAs, which must be disclosed to you as soon as possible. The fees cover any public areas and protection that the HOA might take care of.

Next comes the zoning rules, which will show you what the property is allowed to be used for within the community. For example, if you are purchasing a property in a place where local flora and fauna are abundant, laws and rules may prevent you from building and encroaching on this flora and fauna. These zoning rules might be a deterrent for you to continue with the purchase of the property, so it is important to understand this aspect to make sure you know what you are allowed to do and what you are restricted from.

Finally, you will also have to consider insurance, as many mortgage brokers do not lend money to those who do not have homeowner's insurance. There is no law that suggests you should purchase homeowner's insurance, but it will impact your eligibility to get a mortgage or home loan. Homeowner's insurance is also important to protect you and your home. If anything major were to happen to your property, it would come at a hefty price, so having this insurance would cover these planned situations. The type of homeowner's insurance that you need will depend on the property location and risk factors. For example, if you live in an area where floods are common, then you would need flood insurance tacked on to your insurance policy. Speaking to an insurance broker is the best way to go about this process.

ESTIMATING COSTS FOR RENOVATION DURING PROPERTY ANALYSIS

During the property analysis process, certain areas of maintenance may arise that you will need to address. Your property assessor will look through all the different aspects of the property and then assess whether repairs or renovations are needed. In case you take on repairs, it is important to understand the common renovations when purchasing a property. This could help you mentally prepare should you need to do them. Some of these renovations include roofing, plumbing, electrical work, drywall, pest removal, garbage disposals, and HVAC (Heating, Ventilation, and Air Conditioning) systems.

It can be difficult to estimate the cost of renovations and improvements, but having a roundabout number to work with is important. This is going to help you budget effectively so you can ensure you are renovating properly and have the finances to do so. On top of that, estimating the renovation cost can also help you negotiate with the seller. If there are renovations that are going to cost you a lot and you're willing to do them, then you can negotiate down the price.

Many factors come into play when talking about renovations. The price of a renovation depends on various factors, including the scope of the project, the labor and materials needed, and the duration of the work. You will also need to consider the cost based on your area or region, as labor and supplies vary depending on where you are. The range for any kind of repair or renovation is incredibly wide, so it's not helpful to guess if you do not have specific numbers or know precisely what the renovations are going to entail.

When trying to estimate any kind of renovation, the first thing you need to do is know what renovations will have to be done. You can start researching labor and materials needed for the renovation. It is a good idea to start calling around and contacting the relevant professionals who will be taking care of the renovations. They will send you a quote based on the information you give them, and then you can start comparing quotes. If you have done a home inspection, then you should have a good idea of what needs to be done on the property and can then give this information to the relevant professionals. If you are doing these renovations as an add-on or addition to your property, then you will need to let the professionals who will be doing the renovations know exactly what you are planning to do.

The first person you should get in contact with is a general contractor, as they will be taking care of a majority of the processes. These are the people who have contacts with other relevant professionals in the industry. It may be difficult for you to know who to get into contact with if you do not know what is needed. The general contractor will come in and have a look at your vision and needs, and then both of you can work on a plan going forward and bring in other contractors, such as plumbers and electricians. You are under no obligation to go with the first quote you get, and it is definitely important to shop around so you can find the best deals for your renovations.

INTERACTIVE ELEMENT: DUE DILIGENCE CHECKLIST

Due diligence is an extremely important step when it comes to purchasing a property. You want to ensure you are doing your research to avoid any problems down the line. Here is a checklist you can use for this process.

Pre-offer

- Population growth
- Income levels of households in the area
- Vacancies in the area
- Average and median rent prices
- School ratings
- Property value
- Crime rates

Financial Due Diligence

- Potential gross rental income
- Any other income you could make from the property
- Expenses
- Cost of maintenance and repairs
- Taxes
- Insurance
- Contributions to an emergency savings account for property issues and improvements

Post-offer

- Home inspection by a professional
- Utilities and mechanical systems
- Overall condition of all rooms
- Outside areas, such as the driveway and garden
- Mold and termite inspection
- Flood zone verification

Financial Due Diligence

- Profit/loss statements for two years prior
- Previous owner's income tax return
- Current rent
- Lease terms
- Additional fees charged to renters
- List of repairs and capital improvements
- Existing service contracts
- Taxes

With the property purchase process and renovation planning covered, it's essential to understand the tax benefits and legal considerations of real estate investing. We now go into the third part of the framework.

TELL YOUR STORY TO INSPIRE OTHERS

"If you want to go somewhere, it is best to find someone who has already been there."

— ROBERT KIYOSAKI

The further you get into your journey with real estate investment, the more questions people will have for you. How did you do it? Is it really something that anyone can do? You'll be able to tell them your story and encourage them as they start considering whether they, too, could get started with real estate investment—but unless you decide to dedicate your life to guiding others through the process, you're probably not going to have the time to walk them through every little thing they need to do.

Guiding people through the process has become something of a passion of mine, and it's this that led me to write about both real estate investment and setting up an Airbnb business. I want to make this process as easy and accessible as possible for those with big dreams but little experience, and I want people to realize that this is a much more realistic option than they might have imagined. Essentially, I want to answer all the questions that you're probably going to be asked as you start seeing success with real estate investment... and that means you have a very easy way to help people who are inspired by your journey—all you have to do is point them in the direction of this book!

I'd also like to encourage you to share this book on a wider scale so that I can help more people through this process. All you need to do to make a big difference is leave a short review online.

By leaving a review of this book on Amazon, you'll show new readers exactly where they can find all the information they need to get started with real estate investment—and find a solid route to success.

Reviews are so helpful in connecting books with their intended audiences, and simply by leaving your feedback, you can help others find the information they're looking for quickly. This, combined with any friends or family members you pass this on, will make a huge difference to anyone interested in exploring real estate investment.

Thank you so much for your support. I truly appreciate it.

Scan the QR code below

PART III

PROFIT AND PROSPER

TAX BENEFITS AND LEGAL CONSIDERATIONS

W hen Brendon started his real estate investment journey, something that nobody told him about was the tax benefits. In his first year of running a short-term rental, he brought an accountant on board to help him with the general finances and his taxes since his financial situation had changed. He sat with the accountant, who explained to him the various tax deductions and benefits he could take advantage of through his investments. He was quite surprised as he worked through the list of tax-deductible expenses and items. He never knew that owning an investment property not only increased his income but also reduced his taxable income. This was a big win for him because, like most of us, he's not a big fan of paying unnecessary taxes.

TAX BENEFITS

Real estate investments can help you reduce your taxable income, which is one of the major benefits of investing in real estate. It is important to understand these tax benefits because you don't want to pay more tax than is necessary. Reducing your taxable income means that you have additional finances to put into other areas of your life and even back into your investments. You can speak to a professional accountant or tax advisor for some specific advice, but there are some key areas to be aware of when you are a real estate investor.

One of the most obvious tax benefits of real estate investing is the write-offs that you get with it. A write-off means that you're not taxed on the amount you spend in these areas, which lowers your overall taxable income and results in paying fewer taxes. These tax write-offs include property taxes, insurance, interest on your mortgage, property management fees, and any costs you have to repair or maintain your property. Those are the most common write-offs, but you can also get them if you run your real estate investment as a business since there are business expenses that can be tax write-offs, too. These include business equipment, travel, advertising, fees for legal services, and accounting.

Another tax benefit is depreciation, which is the loss of your property's value over time. If your property produces income, such as a rental property, you will be able to deduct depreciation as an expense and lower your taxable income. You will also have tax benefits through capital gains, which is the amount you will make if you sell your property. This can be divided into short-term and long-term capital gains. Short-term capital gains occur when you buy and sell a property within a year. Long-term capital gains are if you are in possession of the property for more than a year, and capital gains in this category have a much lower tax rate, which is more beneficial to you.

Another wonderful tax benefit that comes with real estate is that if you have rental property and are earning income, you effectively avoid the FICA tax. This payroll tax applies to self-employed individuals who earn an income. If you are self-employed and earn an income through most other avenues, the money you earn is taxed on payroll tax since this person will need to pay for both the employer and the employee portion of the FICA tax. However, if your rental property is considered passive income (as are most long-term rentals), it is not liable for this kind of tax, so you avoid it completely.

1031 EXCHANGE

A tax benefit that needs its own section in this chapter is called the 1031 exchange. This is a strategy in which you defer taxes when you take the profit gained from selling one property and invest in another property. When you take the money out of an investment, you are liable for capital gains tax, but with the 1031 exchange option, you can skip capital gains tax by investing the money from the old property into a new investment property. This is a great way for investors to lower their taxes or at least defer for a significant amount of time.

A process needs to be followed if you want to go this route. The first thing you will need to do is figure out which property you want to sell and which you are going to buy. You have to have properties in mind in order to make the exchange. On top of that, the properties you wish to make this exchange between need to be very similar, even if they're not the same quality and one is more expensive or has a higher value than the other. For example, you would not be able to use the 1031 exchange if you own a one-bedroom apartment and want to exchange it for a vacation home.

This is not the kind of thing that can be done on your own, so you will need an intermediary. This person acts as an exchange facilitator and will handle the transaction. The person or company needs to be qualified, and they will hold your sale in escrow until the exchange has been completed. They will handle most of the process, including coordinating with the seller of the property so they fully understand the implications of the exchange and the process going forward. They will also prepare all the documentation for you and the seller of the new property to make sure the exchange happens successfully and smoothly. The funds from the sale will remain in escrow until the sale is complete, which means the money will be out of your account and be held separately. If everything is successful, the money will be transferred to the seller, but if things don't go according to plan, you will get your money back. They will also guide you through all the paperwork, including the change of title on the deed and property.

There are many requirements for the 1031 exchange, and it is important to understand them before you go through with this process. Firstly, the properties being exchanged need to be of a like kind. You need to ensure that the properties are similar in nature and function for the exchange to occur. Another important consideration is that you will not have access to the proceeds from the sale of your property. If you take any proceeds from the sale, that will be taxable income, and you would not have taken full advantage of the 1031 exchange.

There are timeline requirements that need to be followed in order for this exchange to be successful. First off is the forty-five-day rule. This rule states that you have forty-five days after you sell your property to find a replacement property. You will need to identify this property in writing and include a description of the new property. Then there is the 180-day rule, which specifies you have to close the sale of the replacement property within 180 days of selling your relinquished property. If you do not meet this deadline, you will need to pay capital gains tax on the profit you made from the sale of the initial property you had in your position. Since these timelines are quite short, it may be a good idea to find the exchange property well in advance and start the conversation with the seller of the property. This way, things may go a lot more smoothly, and you will not be at risk of not meeting the deadlines for the 1031 exchange.

LEGAL CONSIDERATIONS

The legal aspects of investing in property are so important. While it might be tempting to skip legal considerations and just throw your money at investments, this is definitely not the most beneficial way to invest in real estate. There are many legal considerations that you will have to contemplate. Knowing what these are is going to help you put your best foot forward.

The first thing you want to do is understand the local regulations where you want to invest. Every city, country, and area is governed by different regulations. This means that what may be legal in one area is completely illegal in another. The local regulations dictate many things, including the type of property development, rental regulations, and zoning laws. Before you even consider investing in a property, ensure you fully understand all local regulations. You can easily find this on the municipality or state's website. If you are concerned about something, then it is worth getting a property lawyer involved to help explain things to ensure you have all the knowledge you need. You definitely don't want to be in the process of making a real estate investment only to realize that you cannot use it in the way you wanted due to overlooked legal considerations.

As you know from Chapter 5, doing your due diligence is essential when it comes to investing in real estate. Legal due diligence has many aspects, but they are all important. The first thing you will need to do is do a title search to make sure that the title is free and that you will be able to take ownership rights of that property. You also need to do a property inspection and survey the property to make sure that you are not being given false information. You want to ensure that you get exactly what you think you'll be getting when you purchase that property. Another part of due diligence is environmental considerations, such as hazards or contaminations. You may need to get a professional involved to evaluate any potential environmental risks currently on the property or that could arise based on what you want to do with your property once you've purchased it.

When you are ready to start negotiating and creating a contract, doing your due diligence in this area is important, too. You definitely don't want to be signing any documents without making sure that you are protected. There will be a lot of paperwork in the process of purchasing a property, and you don't want to overlook any important areas. You can get a real estate lawyer involved to help review contracts and negotiate favorable terms so you are not missing out. There may be potential risks in the contract negotiation that you could miss simply because you do not have all the knowledge. If you choose to go through the process yourself, make sure that you are doing the relevant research and reading through the contract meticulously. If you find a clause or statement that raises a red flag, ensure that you do your research about it and reach out if you need help. It is better to sort this out well in advance rather than being stuck in a contract that is unfavorable to you and your investments.

If your goal is to rent out your property and become a landlord, then it is essential that you understand tenant and landlord laws in the area in which you are investing. You must understand the world and responsibilities of a landlord before you take on that obligation. Being a landlord is not simply renting out your property and then never seeing it again. You have to take care of the maintenance, rental agreement, payments, structure, eviction processes, and any tenancy issues. It is a lot of responsibility, so it is important to understand what you are responsible for and what the tenant's part will be. Knowing this before you become a landlord is important so you can prepare yourself and decide whether you want to do this.

The legal aspects of owning and using a property as an investment are important. You must take the time to understand all legal aspects and do your due diligence in all areas. While this can take some time and effort, you will definitely be thankful that you went through the process. It will save you a lot of time, money, effort, and heartache in the future if you put in the effort now.

Now that we've covered tax benefits and legal considerations, let's discuss generating passive income through rental properties.

PASSIVE INCOME THROUGH LONG-TERM RENTALS

When you're using your real estate investment as passive income, long-term rentals tend to be one of the best options. There are many reasons for this, including the fact that you are making a rental income and earning money through capital growth, getting tax benefits, and diversifying your assets. Taking the time to understand this type of investment strategy is really going to help you see whether it is a good fit for you. Plus, you get to explore the world of rentals and understand the topic at a deeper level.

LONG-TERM RENTALS

A long-term rental is a rental property that you lease out to a tenant for a longer period. These leases can vary in length, but they fall under the umbrella of long-term rental if you are renting out your property to somebody for more than six months.

Benefits

There are many benefits to investing in long-term rentals. Many real estate investors choose to do this due to the benefits and stability it offers. In this section, we are going to talk about the many benefits that come from long-term rentals.

Monthly Rental Income

One of the most obvious benefits is the fact that you are getting a monthly rental income. Since you are renting out the property on a long-term basis, it means that you're making a passive income by getting rental income every month. This stable form of income is predictable and comes in at an agreed-upon date. It allows you to budget and plan, and you know that you are going to get your money.

Depreciation/Tax Deductions

When you own a long-term rental, you have some tax advantages, including writing off certain expenses. For example, you'll be able to write off the interest on your mortgage and depreciation of your assets on your tax forms. This effectively lowers your taxable income, and you will be paying less tax.

Building Equity

If you have a mortgage on your rental property, then you can use your rental income to put toward your mortgage and build equity into your investment. This means that you are paying down the amount you owe so that you own more of the property yourself. You can leverage this equity into other investments or leave it as is, so even if you do have to sell your property before you pay off the entire mortgage, the amount of money you can take out of the property will be a lot more.

Property Appreciation

When a property appreciates in value, it means it is increasing in value over time. Now, there is no guarantee that your property will appreciate in value; however, if you have made a good investment, it is highly likely that your property will increase in value. When you have a rental property, you are making an income from two different areas. The first one is your rental income, and then you're also making money through the property's appreciation in value. While property appreciation might not feel like it is bringing in an income at the moment, when it comes time to sell the property, you will get a lot more than what you purchased it for. You can sell your property for profit when you need to.

Leverage on Investment

If there comes a time when you want to start investing in more than one property or in different kinds of properties, then it is good to know that you can leverage your current properties to do so. You can get a mortgage or loan on a second property by leveraging your first property so that you can get more investments and increase your investment income exponentially. This needs to be done very carefully, as there is a risk when you leverage one property in order to buy more properties. However, if you can make the right investment choices and do your research, you will definitely put yourself in a position for success.

Tips and Tricks

Investing in real estate and rental properties has a learning curve. As you become a more experienced investor, you will learn the nuances that come with this type of investment. With that being said, you want to set yourself up for success from the beginning, so following a few tips and tricks may help you do just that.

Choose the Right Neighborhoods

The neighborhood of the property you want to invest in is going to be crucial for making the most profit. Before you even consider investing in a property, you should do some research on the neighborhood. Even a simple drive through the neighborhood can tell you a lot. An area that is safe and close to good schools, amenities, transportation, shopping centers, and recreational activities is going to be the best neighborhood to invest in.

People always want to live in areas like that, so there will be a demand. When there is a demand for property in an area, a real estate investor can make more money. You will find it a lot easier to find tenants who want to stay in the neighborhood for a long time. When your goal is to make a passive income, getting people who want to live in the neighborhood for an extended period is going to be incredibly beneficial. Many people are willing to rent for five, ten, or even twenty years if they like the neighborhood and want to put down roots there. In this case, you now have a passive stream of income for many years, and you don't have to go through the process of finding new tenants or taking care of a property. Most of the work is done for you, and you can just generate an income.

Locate Profitable Investments

The type of property that you invest in is almost as important as the neighborhood. The property type needs to make sense for the tenant you want to welcome into the home. Properties with more bedrooms and bathrooms will attract bigger families who typically have children. However, smaller properties may attract people who are single or who are just starting out in their lives. This means the amount of money you can charge for rent is going to change. On top of that, how you go about finding your tenants and managing the property is going to differ depending on the type of property you have.

For example, a luxury property will be a little more difficult to market and find tenants for. That is because there is less of a market for luxury properties. However, a single-family home is more appealing to the public, which means it will be a lot easier for you to find tenants. For a beginner investor, a single-family home tends to be the best option. This can be a standalone house, townhouse, or even an apartment.

Look at the Numbers

It is all good to find a beautiful property that you want to invest in, but it is essential that you look at the numbers before you make any kind of investment. The numbers are going to tell you whether the property is going to make a successful investment or if it's going to be a liability. If you have a few properties in mind for your investment, then you can compare the numbers to see which one is going to be the most beneficial investment.

In order to compare the numbers for the different properties, you will need to look at the expenses, cash flow, and potential income from those properties. This is great to assist you in making the best decisions regarding your property investments and ensure that you are not choosing something that will look good on the outside but won't bring in the returns you want.

PRICING STRATEGY

Your pricing strategy is an incredibly important part of your rental investment. If you price your rent too low, it means that you are leaving money on the table, and you might not be making enough to cover your costs. You don't put yourself in a position where you are essentially losing money when making a profit is possible. If you overprice your property, you may end up struggling to find people to rent the space, which will also end up costing you money since you will have vacancies. The goal is to find the sweet spot when it comes to pricing, where you can maximize your profits and ensure you can afford all your expenses.

Know Your Competition

You may have a number in mind that you think you deserve for your rental property, but it is important to know your competition and situate competitively. There is probably a range in which people in the area are willing to pay for property similar to yours. If you set your rent too high, you will put yourself in a position where it is difficult to find tenants. If you set your rent too low, it means that you'll either attract bad tenants or you will be losing money.

Knowing what is going on in your neighborhood will help you set a competitive rate for your rent to maximize your profit and ensure that you have people interested in renting your property. You can go onto property websites to see how much people are charging for rent on properties similar to yours. When doing this research, ensure that you are looking for properties with features and amenities similar to your property. That is what's going to give you the most accurate idea of how much people will pay.

Property prices tend to shift over time, so make sure you check at least every few weeks. This way, you can shift your rental rates to keep your property relevant and competitive in the market.

The 2 Percent Rule Is Just a Guideline

One rule that many landlords tend to stick to is the 2 percent rule. This rule states that you should be charging up to 2 percent of your property's value as rent each month. It makes it easy for you to set a price for monthly rent. This is definitely just a guideline and shouldn't be something that you follow strictly. There is so much to consider when it comes to setting rental prices that it's simply not beneficial for you to stick to this rule without doing any additional research.

Seasonality Matters

You may think that the weather has nothing to do with whether people are looking to rent a property or not, but that is not true. Depending on where you live, there may be differences in seasonality, but the general trend seems to be that people are more likely to move—and look for new properties to live in—during the warmer months. This is probably because it is easier to move when it is warmer. However, in very hot climates, extreme heat can also deter people from relocating. People are generally more willing to stay put in the colder months when they just want to stay indoors. This is especially so if you live in a very cold climate, as it can be incredibly inconvenient and unappealing to move houses in a snowstorm or when children are in the full swing of the school year.

Since the demand for property tends to be lower in the colder months, you may need to price your rent much lower in order to attract potential tenants. If you are going for a long-term rental strategy, this could have a huge negative financial impact on your overall income. If at all possible, you should spend most of your time marketing your property in the summer months so you can get your renters moved in and settled, so you do not have to worry about it in the winter months.

Consider Your Property's Amenities

The price you set for your rental property will not just be based on the property itself. The number of bedrooms and bathrooms is incredibly important, but there are other things that people look for. That is why it is important to consider your amenities, both on the property and in the surrounding area. There are many amenities that people look for and will pay a little extra for. One of these is safe parking. This could be in the form of a garage, assigned parking, or safe street parking. People do not want to park far away and have to walk down the street in order to get home. This means they will be willing to pay a little bit extra if there is safe parking on or close to the property, or if the property is conveniently located near public transit.

Another key aspect is the general safety of the property and the area. If there is some sort of added security, this will give your tenants peace of mind. This kind of security could be a gated community or even smart home technology and security systems installed in the home. People also look at the safety of the general area and whether it is walkable or not. Walkability means that the property is going to be close to local shops and services and that it's safe to walk on the streets.

Another highly beneficial feature that can increase a property's price is outdoor features and entertainment areas. A pool, patio, balcony, or any kind of recreational area is hugely beneficial. This doesn't have to be directly on the property. For example, if there is a tennis court or communal pool nearby or shared by the same cluster of properties, then this will increase your potential rent prices.

TENANT SCREENING

Once you have set up your pricing strategy and are ready to welcome new tenants, it is time to consider the tenant screening process. One of the biggest mistakes that first-time investors make is allowing anyone to rent their property just so they can get an income. Your tenants can make your life much easier or create huge difficulties for you. This is why it is so important to have a robust tenant screening process to ensure you are choosing the right tenants. You want to make sure that the people who live on your property are going to pay on time, take care of your property, and be responsible.

When you put out advertisements for your rental property, you are probably going to get some interest. You should take some time to research all your potential tenants, even though it may be a little more trouble. Certain things are essential to ask your potential tenants about so you can get some data on them to see whether they would be a good fit. With regard to paying their rent on time and being able to afford the rent, you will need their proof of income and creditworthiness. A good rule of thumb is to look for tenants who make more than three times the monthly rent you will be charging. This safe zone shows that your potential tenants can afford to live on the property. It is a good idea to ask for a three- to six-month bank statement to make sure that they have been earning a steady income. In order to check their creditworthiness, you will need to have a look at their credit history and their credit score. If they are good at managing their credit, it means that they are less likely to fall behind with their rent payments and have proven that they managed their finances well.

Next, you will need to check whether they are good people who live responsible lives. You can check their criminal background, eviction history, and their references. You definitely don't want somebody to live on your property who will put the neighbors in danger, so make sure you run a background check to ensure that the potential tenant did not participate in activities that could put your property or people living in the surrounding area at risk. Checking eviction history helps you to see whether this person is a good tenant. Always find out why the tenant was evicted. If it was because of a violation of the lease agreement or any kind of illegal conduct, damages, or missing rent payments, then you know this person may not be a good fit for you. Finally, you will need to have a look at their references, as these will give you a good indication of their character and whether they have been good tenants in the past. It is definitely a red flag if their references don't have anything particularly good to say about them. After the screening process, you will have a much better idea of whether this person is a good fit for you.

SELF-MANAGEMENT VERSUS PROPERTY MANAGEMENT

For managing your rental property, you have two choices. You can either choose to manage it yourself or get a property manager on board to do it for you. Let's start talking about the self-management method and the pros and cons that come with it.

PROS AND CONS OF SELF-MANAGEMENT

Pros

Saving on Fees

Property management comes at a fee, so if you are doing it yourself, you are saving money. You don't have to pay yourself to take care of the property, so you can put this money into other areas of your investment or simply save it for yourself.

Doing Things Yourself

There is something to be said for doing things yourself. You're able to do things your way, and there is no risk of misunderstandings or miscommunications with somebody else. If you enjoy taking on a challenge and doing things yourself, this could be a good route for you.

Choosing Tenants

Managing your property means that you get to be the one to choose the tenants. With a big investment like real estate, there is peace of mind when you make the decisions yourself and choose the tenants based on your own criteria. You can also build a relationship with your tenants that can lead to mutual respect.

Cons

Takes Commitment

Managing a property by yourself takes commitment and a lot of effort. It means you must be available should there be an emergency or if your tenants need you. Many smaller tasks that take up quite a bit of your time need to be taken care of consistently.

Legal Considerations

There are quite a few legalities when it comes to investing in real estate and renting out your property. A property manager will have all the necessary experience that a first-time investor may not have. It will take some extra work on your part to make sure that you understand all the legal processes and requirements so you don't end up in a sticky situation.

Requires Marketing

Doing things yourself also means you will have to market your property yourself. This can be challenging if you have never done it before. On top of that, many property managers have a network that can assist them with finding the right tenants for a property, and an individual investor may not have the same contacts.

Roles of a Property Manager

A property manager deals with many rules and responsibilities. This alleviates a lot of pressure from the investor. Understanding what a property manager does might help you decide whether this is somebody you want to bring onto your team.

Acquiring Tenants

A property manager will be responsible for acquiring the right tenant for the property. If a tenant's lease is up and they decide they no longer want to stay there, the property manager will start the process again and find a new tenant.

Collecting Rent and Handling Evictions

A property manager will also handle the strict tasks of collecting rent and handling any evictions that need to occur. If a tenant is not paying on time, the property manager will start the process of collecting that money and might need to get lawyers and other legal professionals on board. If this situation escalates, then the property manager will also need to handle evictions and all the necessary processes that follow.

Managing Tenant Requests

When you rent out your property, you become a landlord. This means that if anything were to go wrong on the property, the tenants could call you and request that you attend to the issues. If you have a property manager, your tenants will call them should they need anything or have any requests.

Taking Care of Accounting

Accounting is a very important part of managing a property and ensuring that it is running smoothly. Your property manager will take care of all the bookkeeping and make sure that you are making a profit and that money is going into the right areas.

PROS AND CONS OF PROPERTY MANAGEMENT

Now that you know what a property manager does, it is important to know the pros and cons. This will give you a broader understanding of property management so you can see both sides of the coin.

Pros

Easy and Stress-Free

Hiring a property manager means that the rental process is going to be a lot easier for you. You will not need to stress out about your tenant's maintenance of the property or any other aspect of being a landlord. You will only need to get involved if something very important requires your attention, and your property manager will contact you regarding this.

Understand the Market

Property managers will have experience in the real estate market, and that means they can make decisions with a wealth of knowledge. This might be something you do not have, so bringing this kind of professional on board could help you see better returns on your investment.

Build a Wall Between You and the Tenants

If you are the type of person who does not want to deal with the social aspects of having tenants, then a property manager is a great choice. It creates a barrier between you and your tenants, so you do not have to deal with them or have any direct contact with them.

Oversee Maintenance and Problems

Running a rental property means that maintenance needs to be taken care of and problems need to be solved. The property manager will call the tenant if there is a problem or if maintenance is needed in a certain area. The manager will also handle all maintenance schedules and ensure your property runs smoothly throughout the year.

Cons

Poor Performance

There is always a risk that your property manager will perform poorly and not meet your expectations. Therefore, it is essential to choose the right property manager, but sometimes, things go wrong, even with all the right steps being taken.

Troublesome Employees

When hiring a property manager, you are essentially relinquishing a lot of control to that person. This means they can hire staff or contractors to help with the maintenance, cleaning, and anything else on the property. There's always a risk of troublesome employees working on your property, and sometimes, this could even be the property managers themselves.

Loss of Revenues

When hiring a property manager, you have to pay them for their services. This is typically a percentage of your rent or revenue. The percentage will vary depending on the property manager or the company they work for. Often, this is somewhere between 5 and 10 percent.

Pay for Fees

On top of the percentage payment that you owe them, there may also be additional fees you need to pay. Some property management companies require a placement fee if they find a new tenant for your property. It is important to understand the contract when working with a property manager so you know what costs you might be liable for.

IDEAS TO GENERATE MORE INCOME FROM YOUR RENTAL PROPERTIES

You can make some additional income from your rental property in many ways. Some investors choose to stick to the basics and just generate revenue through the rent they charge, but you can get a little creative and expand your money-making opportunities. These ideas are not going to work for every property or for every investor.

However, you can try one or two of these options to increase the revenue you make through your rental properties.

Rent out fully furnished apartments and rooms. You can charge a bit more when you are renting out fully furnished apartments and rooms. People are more willing to spend when a living space is aesthetically decorated and taken care of.

Offer storage space. If you have additional space in your garage or spare room, you can offer it as a storage space. People are always looking for places to store their extra furniture and items.

Minimize resident turnover. If you are trying to ensure that your property makes the most profit, it is important to minimize your turnover. If you have long-term tenants, it means that you are getting a steady rental income without having to do much work. This means you must provide them with excellent service and ensure that you meet their needs.

Add services and amenities. See if you can add a service or amenity that could be beneficial to your tenants. For example, you could offer a laundry or cleaning service since this is something that people often need. You can add additional amenities like a pool, play area, or air conditioning to add greater benefits to your property.

Reinvest your profits. The money you make from your rental doesn't need to be spent immediately. Instead, you can use this money to reinvest to continue growing your profits. Even though you may not be using the money you're making immediately, you are increasing your overall net worth, and it will be valuable in the future.

Use dynamic pricing strategies. A dynamic pricing strategy means you change your prices based on what is going on in the market. If you are trying to find tenants when there is a lot of demand, then you can increase your prices since people will be willing to pay more. You can decrease your price and offer a discount to be more attractive and competitive in the quieter season.

Increase energy efficiency. Electricity and energy cost a lot of money, so get an energy professional into your property to see how you can use energy more efficiently. This can save you a lot of money in the long run, and it is also kinder to the environment.

INTERACTIVE ELEMENT: CREATING A PROPERTY MANAGEMENT PLAN

Creating a property management plan is crucial when it comes to running a rental property. Without a plan, things can get overlooked, and this will make things harder for you in the future. Follow these steps to create a robust property management plan.

Step 1: Taking Care of Your Property's Needs

Property's existing issues:

_____

_____

_____

Trends in the local rental market:

_____

_____

_____

Legal requirements:

_____

_____

_____

Step 2: Setting Goals

Long-term goals:

_____

_____

_____

Short-term goals:

_____

_____

_____

Financial goals:

_____

_____

_____

Tenant satisfaction goals:

_____

_____

_____

Property-specific goals:

_____

_____

_____

Step 3: Create Your Budget

Income:

Name	Amount

Expenses:

Name	Amount

Savings:

Name	Amount

Step 4: Make a Maintenance Schedule

Indoors:

Name	Budgeted Amount	Date

Outdoors:

Name	Budgeted Amount	Date

Plumbing:

Name	Budgeted Amount	Date

Electrical:

Name	Budgeted Amount	Date

Landscaping:

Name	Budgeted Amount	Date

HVAC:

Name	Budgeted Amount	Date

Other Upkeep:

Name	Budgeted Amount	Date

Now that you're familiar with long-term rentals, let's move on to short-term rentals and why they're profitable.

SHORT-TERM RENTALS

Active listings on Airbnb exceeded 7.7 million by the end of 2023, increasing 18 percent year-over-year with sustained double-digit supply growth across all regions. And in 2023 alone, hosts earned more than $57 billion (Airbnb, 2024). This shows how much money there is to be made through short-term rentals and platforms like Airbnb. If you have not considered short-term rentals, then this may be your sign to start thinking about it.

WHAT ARE SHORT-TERM RENTALS?

A short-term rental is also known as a vacation rental. It is a property the owner rents out to people who will only stay there for a short period. The property must be fully furnished, and all necessary amenities must be provided to the guests. With short-term rentals, we refer to the people staying in the property as guests rather than tenants because they are not staying there on a long-term basis. The guests are also not responsible for taking care of the property in the ways a tenant would. There are completely different expectations between the two, and the goal of a short-term rental business is to make sure there are consistent bookings of the property.

Short-term rental properties are a growing market. We are seeing it become more and more accessible through companies like Airbnb and VRBO. These are platforms where somebody with a property posts it as a listing, and people looking for a short-term rental can easily view and book. It is an alternative to a hotel so that guests can get a unique experience as well as competitive pricing. A host, or the owner of the property, also has a good chance to make even more money than with a long-term rental. This is because people are willing to pay more per night when they are booking a vacation or short-term stay. If you have good guest turnover, you will have a high chance of making good money through short-term rentals. As with anything, short-term rentals have pros and cons, and it's important to understand these before diving in.

PROS

Flexibility

There is a lot of flexibility in how you choose to run a short-term rental. If you only want to rent out your property on certain days, then you can do that. You can bring in guests as often or as seldom as you would like. Some people choose to rent their homes or their main property on a short-term rental basis when they are traveling. For example, if you plan a two-month European vacation, you can rent out your home to make additional money while you're not there. Another example of this flexibility would be if you have a rental property that is a bit farther away from you and you are only in the area on the weekends. You could choose to rent out your property on the weekends when you can attend to your guests, and it's most convenient for you.

Most of the short-term rental platforms and websites allow you to choose when you want to rent out your property. If there is a time when you do not want to accept guests, you can block that out on the calendar so people cannot book. This gives you complete control over when you are accepting guests and when it is going to be the most convenient for you.

Higher Cash Flow

With short-term rentals, you have the opportunity to make a lot of money. All you have to do is a bit of quick math to figure this out. A property could bring in $1,500 per month for rent on a long-term basis. Renting out a property as a vacation rental allows you to charge $1,500 for a week. That means you could potentially earn four times as much money using a short-term rental strategy.

The reason for this huge difference in pricing is that when you set a fee for a short-term rental, you are doing it on a per-night basis. But for a long-term rental, you have to set a per-month rental price that must be locked in for the duration of the lease. Something else to consider with short-term rentals is that you can change the nightly fee whenever you want. When vacation properties are in high demand, you can increase the price in order to generate more profit. You can also lower the price in the low-demand seasons to attract more people to your vacation rental. There are a lot of pricing strategies that you can use when it comes to short-term rentals that are simply not available with a long-term rental. This maximizes the amount of profit that you can make.

Fewer Tenant Legal Disputes

With a short-term rental, there is a lower likelihood of you having large legal disputes with your guests. A guest will typically stay for no longer than a week and then move on. However, with a long-term tenant, there are a lot of legal aspects to take into consideration. A prolonged tenant and landlord relationship can lead to legal action based on disagreements. These kinds of legal disputes can be costly as well as time-consuming.

It is important to note that there are tenant laws that protect short-term renters in the same way they might protect long-term rentals. Staying up-to-date with all the relevant property laws will make your life a lot easier in the long run. You will cover your back and ensure that you are meeting all the relevant legal standards.

CONS

Risk of Prolonged Vacancy

There are risks when it comes to short-term rentals. While the potential for a larger income is definitely there, there is also the risk of a prolonged vacancy. When this happens, you will not be making any money through rental income for the duration of the vacancy. There is no guarantee that you will get consistent bookings and guests. With a vacation rental, you have to understand the market. Some months are booming, and people are booking their vacations like crazy, while other months are much slower. In the slower months, you may struggle to get people to book with you, which means that you will be losing out.

With a prolonged vacancy, you will still be liable for the utilities on the property. With a long-term rental, the tenants have to pay the utilities, but this is not the case with a short-term rental. You will have to pay the mortgage and any other bills that come with the property, even if you're not making money at that moment. If there are prolonged vacancies, you will also need to make more of an effort to go and check on the property, as there is no one there to report potential issues like plumbing problems, damages, or electrical faults.

In seasons when there are not a lot of bookings, it is still important for you to maintain the general cleanliness of the property. You don't know when you will get new guests, and making a good impression is important. That means that even if nobody is in the property, you still have to make sure it is up to standard.

More Time and Property Upkeep

Since the guest turnover in a vacation rental property is high, you are required to spend more time on your rental property. This is not a passive income because you have to turn over the property and ensure it's ready for your next guest. When one guest checks out, you have to go in, clean the property, and make sure all the necessities have been replaced. Then, you will need to check in the new guests and make sure they have everything they need. You also have to be on call should your guests need something from you or have an emergency.

With short-term rentals, the goal is to give your guests the best experience possible. You will only get guests and have good ratings on the platform if you provide exceptional service. This means you will need to be there for your guests and provide them with the service they want.

You may also need to do regular maintenance and upkeep checks more often. Some guests may not be as careful as you would like them to be. Remember that when guests check into a place for a holiday, they don't want to think about anything serious. Their main goal is to relax or have fun. In that case, they might be a bit more careless with handling things, which means more maintenance is going to be required from you. Of course, they shouldn't destroy your property, but if they are a little clumsy with their luggage or decide to move around the furniture, then there will be scuffs and scratches that you may need to take care of. With long-term rentals, a lot of these minor issues need to be taken care of by the tenant, but this is not the case with short-term rentals.

Fewer Tenant Screening Options

With a short-term rental, the primary goal is to get as many people in and out quickly as possible. That is how you are going to make the most money. However, this does mean you do not have the opportunity to screen your tenants as you would in a long-term rental. At the start of your short-term rental endeavor, you may accept any potential guest who wants to book with you just so you can make some money and get some reviews on the rental platforms.

Some screening and security measures have been implemented with platforms such as Airbnb and VRBO. However, this is not a comprehensive screening process. It verifies basic information like a phone number, email address, and government ID. Then, there are reviews on the platform that you can check out. Just as a guest can rate and review you on the platform, the people who own the properties can write and review those who stay with them. It is always a good idea to look at these ratings and reviews to ensure that the person hasn't been destructive or inconsiderate. However, in many cases, the person may not have reviews, which means you won't have those to rely on when accepting their booking. There is always a chance that you will get a problematic guest who could cause damage to the property and violate the house rules you have set up.

INTERACTIVE ELEMENT: ARE SHORT-TERM RENTALS
FOR YOU?

If you are considering the short-term rental option, then it is good to understand whether the pros outweigh the cons for you. The best way to do this is to note the cons and see how you can navigate them. Write down the cons you are most concerned about and then come up with one or two ideas that will mitigate the risks of those cons.

_____

_____

_____

_____

_____

Short-term rentals are important to consider as a real estate investment strategy. They can make you a steady income and help you reach financial freedom. One way to operate short-term rentals is through Airbnb. We will be discussing Airbnb as an investment strategy in more detail in the next chapter.

THE AIRBNB OPPORTUNITY

Out of all these short-term rental platforms out there, Airbnb is definitely the most popular and has the furthest reach. Like many other short-term rental property sites, Airbnb is essentially designed like a marketplace. This marketplace connects people looking for accommodation with people renting out their property on a short-term basis. It has created a way for people to make additional money, and it helps people looking for a vacation find unique places at a cheaper price.

It is fairly easy to sign up on the platform. Once you have created an account and uploaded all the relevant information, you can post your listing. From here, people will be able to view your listing when they are looking for a vacation rental in the area. You have full control of when you want to rent out your property and have access to a calendar where you can open up or block out specific dates. You will also be able to chat with people who are interested in renting out your property.

Airbnb also allows you to advertise unique stays and experiences. If there is something extra special about your property or it can offer an uncommon experience, then you'll be able to advertise this as something separate. For example, if you have access to horse riding or boating cruises, you could advertise these on the platform, too.

I have written books on Airbnb and short-term rentals that could help you gain further insights into the topic. There are lots of details and information that need to be considered when you are working through a platform like Airbnb. Not to mention the tips, tricks, and hacks you can use to increase your revenue and ensure the process is as smooth as possible. If this interests you, I highly suggest you pick up one of my other books so you can set yourself up for success when it comes to your Airbnb or short-term rental.

Before diving into this topic, it is important to take into account the legal regulations surrounding Airbnb. You don't want to pay any unnecessary fees or penalties down the road. As an Airbnb host, it is really important that you understand the laws in your city, country, state, or territory. You will need to get this advice directly from your government or municipality and keep checking back regularly for any changes. You can also check the Airbnb help center, which should offer some guidance for your city. You should also visit your local government website to see the permits or licenses needed to start a short-term rental business. Some things to look into are business licenses, building codes, zoning rules, permits, tax laws, and landlord-tenant laws. With that being said, let's go through some of the basics when it comes to using Airbnb.

Creating an Airbnb Account

The great thing about Airbnb is that it is incredibly easy to create an account. First, you will need to log onto the Airbnb website and choose the sign-up option. You will be guided step-by-step through the process by the use of prompts and forms.

In order to have an active Airbnb account, you will need to verify your account, and this usually requires your government-issued ID. You also need to upload a photo for facial recognition. Once you have done that, you will have to wait up to twenty-four hours for Airbnb to review and verify your information. Once you have done that, you will be approved on the Airbnb site and can continue to build your profile.

Listing a Property, Including Niche Options

There are many steps to take when listing a property on the Airbnb site. It is highly important that you do this properly because it is the only way that you get to market yourself on the website. When you first start listing your property, you must go through various steps to present the most accurate information. Remember, not all guests are looking for the same type of property or vacation, so being specific about what you have to offer is really important.

The first thing you must do to list your property is select your property type. There are different options for property types on the Airbnb website. Currently, the options are an apartment, house, self-contained unit, unique space, bed-and-breakfast, or boutique hotel. Have a look at your property and the space you offer and see which category suits it. You can rent out a room or even part of your home, so you are not just limited to the traditional versions of the above categories. Once you have selected your property type, you will then continue to get a little more specific. There are many options, including niche options. Whatever options you choose, just make sure that you are being honest and truthful because you want to manage your guest's expectations.

You will further categorize based on the type of space you will rent out. There are three options that you can choose from. The first is an entire home or apartment, which is pretty self-explanatory. With this option, you rent out the entire apartment or space for your guests to use. That means that any guest renting out the space will expect to have all the amenities you would find in a regular home or apartment. For example, they will look for things like a kitchen, laundry facilities, cooking utensils, and cleaning supplies. Think about a family or large group coming to stay for a while and what they would need. The next type is a shared room, which is when your guest will be sharing a room with another guest or guests. This is more like a hostel where multiple guests can stay together. The guest would expect to have shared amenities and rooms. Finally, you can have a private room where the guest would have their own private room or space, but other areas of the space will be shared with other people.

Once you have handled the type of property, you'll need to move on to selecting your location. Make sure your location is as accurate as possible because your guests will book primarily based on location. Your guests will not get your exact address until you have approved their stay and are in contact with them, but there will be a map that will give them a very general idea of where your property is.

You will need to specify how many bedrooms and bathrooms you have available, as well as the amenities. You will also need to indicate how many guests you will allow to book at once to ensure a comfortable stay.

You will then need to start taking some photos of your property to upload to the Airbnb website. This is highly important because people seek out potential vacation rentals with their eyes. If your pictures are eye-catching and interesting, then you will probably get more potential guests interested in your space. Ensure that you are taking clear pictures in good lighting. You can even get a professional photographer to assist you with getting excellent pictures of your property. You also want to ensure the property is neat and there is no unnecessary clutter when taking the pictures. Essentially, you want to put your best foot forward when you are snapping those pics.

Another important aspect of listing your property on the Airbnb website is creating a title and adding a description. The title will give anyone scrolling through the Airbnb listings a quick idea of what your property offers. Remember to choose your words carefully and be truthful. Once you've got your title, you can move on to creating a description, which is a lot more detailed. You can have a look at other Airbnb listings to get an idea of what descriptions work best. Make sure you supply a list of the features and benefits of your property. There is a rather large word count allotted for the description, so make sure you are being as detailed as possible.

At this point, your listing is almost ready to go, so you need to think about pricing. For a beginner, the best way to go about it is to do some research on similar Airbnb listings in your area to see what other people are charging. When you first start, you will need to price your rental competitively to get people to book with you. The more reviews you have and the more people who have stayed at your property, the easier it is going to be to find more guests. Remember to be realistic with your pricing and that you can always change it as time goes on. When you are more established, you can increase your nightly rate to be fairly compensated. Remember to also take into consideration things like the type of rental you have, the time of year, and your location. All of these will play a big role in your pricing strategy. It is a good idea to continuously do research and look at other Airbnb listings so you know how to price your property competitively.

It is good to note that you can save your listing without publishing it and come back and fill in the rest of the details later. Since it is a fairly comprehensive listing, it can take quite a long time, and you don't have to do it all in one sitting. Once you fill in all this information, you will need to answer some questions, and then you can publish your listing to the public. All that's left now is to watch the bookings roll in.

Setting Competitive Prices

I've already mentioned how important a competitive pricing strategy is. You will need to set yourself up for success, and you can do that by taking the right steps toward pricing your property correctly. First, you will want to figure out how much your Airbnb costs you per night. This is the base from where you will work out how much you are going to charge as a nightly rate. You should aim to make a profit or at least break even. Your nightly cost will need to include your rent, utilities, taxes, and any other costs that factor into running your Airbnb or owning your property. Since a lot of the bills and expenses are calculated on a monthly basis, you can simply take your monthly costs and divide them by thirty in order to get your nightly costs.

Now that you know exactly how much your Airbnb is costing you, it is time to think about how much profit you want to make. The rate you set should be higher than the nightly rate you spend on your Airbnb. You also have to take into consideration other things, such as the time you are spending to manage your Airbnb. This may not be a solid monetary value, but you are adding value to the guest and, therefore, need to charge for it. Make sure you do market research and look at how much other Airbnbs are charging for a similar service to what you offer. Even if you have decided on a price for your nightly rate, you need to adjust for the current market. If you are overcharging, it means people will not choose you as their first option. You are probably going to lose out on potential bookings because of this. If you are undercharging, it means that you are leaving money on the table and not optimizing your potential income.

Airbnb also has a smart pricing tool that you can either turn on or off. This tool will automatically shift your price up and down, depending on what is happening in the market. The algorithm will look at the demand for properties similar to yours and then determine a price to set per night. You can also set a minimum nightly rate that the smart pricing tool cannot go below so that you still have some control over your nightly rates. If you do not want to price your listing manually, then this is definitely a good option.

Managing Bookings Remotely

You may not be available to be at your property whenever guests check in and book with you. Perhaps you have multiple Airbnb properties, or maybe you are just not in town when you are going to have guests staying with you. Having a strategy to handle your bookings and guests remotely can give you much more flexibility when you are an Airbnb host.

COMMUNICATE WITH YOUR GUESTS

Communication is always going to be key when you are managing any kind of rental. Airbnb tracks how quickly you respond to your guests, and this shows up on your listing profile. It is even more important to prioritize communication with your guests if you will not be there in person to welcome them or have an in-person conversation with them.

You should focus on communicating with your guests before, during, and after check-in and their stay. You also want to make sure that you give your guests all the necessary information. You can also check in with your guests periodically throughout the day, depending on how long their stay is. You definitely don't want to overcommunicate while they stay on your property, as this can get highly annoying. Instead, check in on them once or twice, and then make sure you're easily reachable should they need you. Check in with them to see how they enjoyed their stay, and always ask if they are willing to give you a good review on the platform.

Set Up Automated Messaging

Life can get busy, so it is a good idea to set up some sort of auto-mated message in case you cannot respond at a certain time. This message can be a welcome to your guests and provide them with all the information they need. You can also set up automatic replies to guest questions, which will help your guests get the answers they need without you having to be involved.

Set Plenty of Reminders

You will have many different responsibilities when you are an Airbnb host, so make sure to set reminders on your calendar so you do not get distracted or forget. If you have a guest checking in or you need to do maintenance on the property, set this in your calendar as a priority for you to do.

Solicit Guest Reviews

Solicitation sounds like a bad word, but it is important to always ask for a review. Sometimes, guests do forget, and getting good reviews bumps you up on the platform and puts you in a better position to find more potential guests. You can ask for a review a few days after your guests have checked out, and you can even send an automated message for this to happen. Remember to be polite when asking for a review, as this will increase your chances of getting a positive one.

Offer Self-Check-In

These days, a lot of technology is available to make a short-term rental owner's life easier. You can implement a self-check-in system so your guests can check in without you having to be there. This is a lot more convenient for both of you since you do not have to coordinate check-in times based on availability. One option for a self-check-in would be a lockbox where you leave the key to the property and give the guest a code to access the box. You can also change the property's locks to digital locks that open with a code, fingerprint, or password. You can then change this code or password for each guest, which is an additional level of security.

Get Home Security

Since you are welcoming people into your property, it is essential that you have a home security system. You will not be on the property often enough to make sure that it is safe and secure. You want to ensure your home is secure and your guests are safe. Installing security cameras and other security systems can be very helpful. If you are installing security cameras, be aware that Airbnb has strict rules surrounding the location of the cameras. They can be outside, but no cameras are allowed inside the home or property.

Make House Rules Clear

With Airbnb, you set the house rules, so make sure these are clear to your guests before they check in. You can send out the house rules to them in advance, but then also have a printed version of the house rules in the home. Some Airbnb hosts choose to put the relevant rules in the specific areas of the house. For example, if it is a non-smoking area, you can put up signs around the property to ensure that your guests know the rules and restrictions.

Compose a Guest Book

A guest book is a great way to show your guests that you care and provide them with all the information they need to enjoy their stay. This guest book can include things like instructions for the property and how-to manuals for the amenities and technology. You can also include the house rules as well as tips and tricks for enjoying their stay. Some Airbnb hosts go above and beyond and include local attractions and features in the area that guests may enjoy experiencing.

Organize a Welcome Gift

Another way to personalize your guest experience is to have a welcome gift ready for them when they check in. Since you will not be there in person, this is a nice touch that you can add to make a guest feel welcome. You can add whatever you want to this welcome pack, but making sure that it's on theme and will be useful to your guests is important. For example, you can include some local treats, important toiletries they may need, and even a friendly note for them.

Handling Guest Inquiries

One thing that will make your life so much easier is if you can anticipate your guests' questions and answer them before they even ask. That way, you do not have to go back and forth with questions and answers that could have easily been resolved from the get-go. On top of that, it is best to have your answers locked and loaded so you can give your guests accurate information if you are on the phone with them or communicating with them through email or on the Airbnb app. You can even have answers to common questions drafted out so you can simply copy and paste them, which makes it a lot easier. Below are a few of the most common questions that guests ask and some tips on how to answer them correctly.

Where Is the Property Located?

While the address will be given to your guests as soon as you accept them and they pay, it is still important to understand that some guests do not read all the details and may ask this question.

On top of the address, they will probably want to know how far it is from the amenities and the airport, as well as the directions from the airport to your property. You may also want to add some additional details on how to find your property, like the name of the building or any landmarks that could stand out to them.

Can We Check In or Out Early?

For the sake of convenience, some guests will ask if they can check in or out earlier or later than usual. Whether you accept earlier check-in or later check-out is up to you and is dependent on your schedule. If you have guests back to back, it might be difficult to accommodate these custom check-in and check-out times because you have to turn over the property and ensure it's clean and ready to go. If you cannot clean up and have the property ready for your next guest in a shorter amount of time, then it's best to let your guests know that you cannot accommodate a different check-in or check-out time. This is far better than letting them check into an untidy apartment or having the cleaning staff or you running up and down trying to get things ready while they are in the property. However, if you can accommodate them, your guests will appreciate it.

Does Your Property Have This Item?

Sometimes, guests will inquire about whether or not you have a certain item or amenity for them to use when they get to your property. To save time, you can have a list of all the items and amenities saved so you can easily send it to your guests or copy and paste this list into a message should they ask about a specific item. It is also a good idea to take as many pictures as possible of the important areas of your house so they can see what kinds of amenities and items are available.

What About a Discount?

You can't blame a guest for trying to get a discount so they can pay a little bit less. With that being said, you are under no obligation to give your guests a discount. However, you might consider selecting certain people to give discounts to under special circumstances. For example, if guests are staying for a longer time, you can offer a discount. You may also want to consider giving a discount to regular and loyal guests. Another good way to use a discount is to offer them at specific times of the year, like New Year celebrations, Christmas, or just when there is less demand in your area.

Can I Bring Someone Over, Such as a Family Member or a Friend?

Sometimes, a guest may want to invite other people over to the Airbnb once they have arrived. Sometimes, it is just for a visit, and others invite other people to stay with them. You should make sure that you are clear about your rules and policies surrounding the number of guests that are going to be on your property. Some guests want to have parties in the Airbnb, and this could get unruly and cause damage to your property. If you do not want parties in your Airbnb, then clearly state this in the rules. If you allow your guests to bring over other people, make sure they know the perimeters, such as how many guests can visit and when they need to leave.

Maintaining the Property

Maintenance is one of the most important things you can do for your property. When you run an Airbnb, it means there will be a lot of traffic in and out of your home. Maintenance is of the utmost importance because it shows that the house meets the standards your guests require and that you are not leaving things too long before you start making fixes and changes. Having a schedule and list can help you stay on track with your maintenance. That way, you won't accidentally forget something.

Some things need to be done weekly. You will find a list of those things below.

- Inspect all plumbing and water sources for leaks.
- Wash windows and doors and inspect for cracks or damages.
- Double-check that all the locks in the house are working correctly.
- Check furniture.
- Check that all safety systems and fire extinguishers still work.
- Check for any indication of pests.
- Do a general clean and tidy up of the house.
- Test all remote controls and electronic devices.
- Check electrical outlets and light fixtures.
- Ensure all items are packed away where they need to be.

Becoming a Superhost

The title of Superhost is coveted among Airbnb hosts. Before we get into the rest of the topic, it is important to know what a Superhost is. A Superhost is somebody who has an above-average rating due to exceptional service and the provision of amazing guest experiences. When you get to Superhost status, you will get a badge displayed on your profile so that everybody can see it on the listing page. You can also charge a good amount more because you are reliable and now have an elevated status on the platform.

There are a few criteria that you need to meet in order to become a Superhost. The first criterion is that you have a minimum of three stays, which equals up to one hundred nights stayed, or a minimum of ten trips or reservations booked with you. You will also need to ensure that you keep the standard of a 90 percent response rate to potential guests who have questions or are looking to book with you. Your cancellation rate needs to be under one percent to show that you don't just cancel on your guests whenever you feel like it. Another incredibly important criterion is that you have a review score of 4.8 or more.

Once you have met all of these criteria, then you will be considered a Superhost. This is not something that you need to apply for. Instead, this is awarded automatically once you have met all the criteria. The review process takes place once every quarter, so you have a chance to be awarded a Superhost badge every three months. If, for any reason, you no longer meet the criteria, your badge will be removed, and you will need to work your way back up to being a Superhost.

INTERACTIVE ELEMENT: PLAN YOUR FIRST AIRBNB LISTING

Having a plan to start your very first Airbnb is so important. You must plan your listing and get everything in order before jumping in. I have written two books on becoming a successful Airbnb host. These could be essential reading should you want to become an Airbnb host.

You can find these by scanning the QR code below:

You can also get in touch with other people in the Airbnb community. More experienced people will be able to share a wealth of knowledge with you. I have created a Facebook group just for this purpose. I would encourage you to join and get an inside look at the world of Airbnb. Here are the details:

Name: Airbnb Host Community
URL: www.facebook.com/groups/airbnbhostcommunity
QR Code:

After exploring Airbnbs, it's now time to focus on long-term success and wealth-building strategies. In the next chapter, we will explore how to ensure sustainable growth and maximize your real estate investments over time.

LONG-TERM SUCCESS AND WEALTH-BUILDING

"Real estate cannot be lost or stolen, nor can it be carried away. Purchased with common sense, paid for in full, and managed with reasonable care, it is about the safest investment in the world."

— FRANKLIN D. ROOSEVELT

PROPERTY REHAB

Property rehab is simply rehabilitating a property that may be in poor condition to make it live up to its full potential. You are essentially going to be restoring a piece of real estate to increase its functionality and appearance and raise the value of that property. There are many steps to consider when you do this, but it can be worth it if you do it right.

Property Condition Assessment

The first thing you will need to do is assess the property's current condition. This will give you a starting point so you can identify any big issues that need your attention. Ensure you do this assessment thoroughly and get professionals involved when necessary. You definitely don't want to be shocked by an enormous expense down the road.

Create a Checklist

Once you have done your assessments, you need to organize all of your information into a checklist. This will help you easily work through each thing that needs to be done for the renovation project. Doing this ensures that you understand the task at hand and keeps everything organized so you don't accidentally miss something.

Make a Budget

When it comes to real estate, everything costs money, so it is important to have a budget. Based on your checklist, try to figure out the estimated amount that you would need for each item. You also need to be prepared for emergencies and unforeseen expenses. Sometimes, you just don't know the full cost of something until you do it, so it is important to have some cushioning in your budget.

Find a Contractor

A good contractor will save you a lot of money but also a lot of time and stress. Choose a contractor with a lot of experience and a good track record. You also want to make sure the contractor you choose has experience with the type of renovations and improvements you are doing to your property.

Debris and Trash Removal

This is by no means the most glamorous part of the process, but you will need to organize the removal of any debris or trash on the property. This is not just for aesthetic purposes but for safety reasons as well. Accidents can happen if there are random items lying around. Depending on how much trash and debris is on the property, you may need to hire a service to assist you.

Interior Renovations

The most exciting part of any kind of rehabilitation or revamp of a property is probably the decorating, but you cannot start there. You first need to take care of structural issues and any other major problems before you move on to the design aspects. These are what's going to cost you the most money, and they may also be safety concerns. Dealing with this first is in the best interests of everybody who takes up residence on this property.

Work on the Exterior

The exterior of the house is also important because you want to increase curb appeal. The outside of the property is the first thing people see, so if you can draw them in from the get-go, you have a much better chance of increasing the value and getting people interested in either purchasing your property or renting it out from you. Take care of the lawn and exterior of the home and anything they can see from the street view.

Finalize the Project

Now is the time to do a walk-through to ensure all the work has been carried out to your liking. Don't simply trust your contractors or other people to approve everything. It is important for you to be involved in the finalizing process and make sure that you check everything thoroughly.

SELLING YOUR PROPERTY

There are many reasons why you may want to sell your property. It could be due to a life event, or it could be a strategic decision. There is no right or wrong answer to the question of when to sell your property, but you need to think about it before you do it. It is a big decision, and you want to make sure that you are thinking it through and considering all the options before you go through with the sale.

Below are some reasons why you might sell your property:

- In the case of a major life event, you may no longer be able to handle the maintenance or responsibility of the property.
- Your other investments bring in more income than this one.
- Your cap rate is sitting below the risk-free rate of return.
- You no longer find joy in owning this property but find it in something else that is more important to you.
- Other options may be more lucrative for your investments, and you want to explore those.
- The tax laws have changed, and now homeowners are getting stuck with excessive taxes.
- Your property is simply too expensive for you to handle at this moment.
- You no longer want to own this property for a personal reason.

As you can see, there are many reasons why somebody might not want to own a specific piece of property any longer. If you have considered it and examined all your options, it is perfectly okay to look into selling your property.

If you have decided that selling your property is the best way forward, it is important to think about ways to maximize your profit from the sale. One of the best ways to do this is to avoid as many taxes as possible when selling your property. There are various ways in which you can do that, and one way is through something called tax harvesting. In order to do this, you will be offsetting your capital gains with losses so that you can reduce the amount you are paying in tax. For example, if you see that your property has increased in value over the years, but you have other investments that have decreased in value, you can sell the other investments at a loss so you can balance out your overall capital gains and pay less tax. You could also use a 1031 exchange to reduce the amount you are paying in tax. As mentioned, you can use this exchange to purchase a similar property to avoid capital gains taxes. You could also use Section 121 exclusion, with which you can exclude up to a maximum amount of $500,000 if you are married and filing jointly on your capital gains. You can only do this by converting an investment property into your and your spouse's primary residence. If you are a single person, then this will be cut in half, and the benefit is $250,000.

When selling your rental property, there are other things to consider to increase the amount you will get from the sale. While considering capital gains tax is important, it's not the be-all and end-all. One of the best things you can do is to hire a professional who understands real estate investing and can help you through the process. This may result in you saving so much money in the long term that it will be worth it. You should also consider completing any repairs, renovations, or upgrades you had in the works. Even some repairs or renovations make a significant difference in the selling price of your property. You also need to ensure you are marketing your property well to attract buyers with money to spend. These are key to getting the price you deserve when you are selling your current real estate.

REINVESTING PROFITS

Once you have determined that selling your property is the best for you and you have received some profit, you need to decide what you will do with that profit. It may seem tempting for you to spend as much of it as possible. However, this is not usually the best way to go. Reinvesting that profit into other investment types is a much better long-term approach. You have already worked hard to build up your current real estate investment and make a profit, and you don't want to lose it by making a few bad purchasing decisions.

There are many things that you could invest your money into. With real estate, so many options are available that it is difficult to choose just one. Diversifying your investments is one of the best things you can do for the health of your future portfolio and to ensure you make the most profit possible. If you haven't already looked into a REIT, then this is the time to do so. This is a way that you can invest your money into real estate without being an active participant in managing your property. We have already done a deep dive into this kind of investment, so if you want a recap, it is best to go back to Chapter 1 and get all the information you need.

You can also diversify your investment portfolio through different types of real estate. If you have sold a property and are looking to invest in real estate differently, there are many categories you can look into. You can look into the geographical location of the properties you invest in. If all of your real estate investments are in one area, you can expand this by purchasing in a different city or even state. It does mean you will need to do some research on the state laws when it comes to real estate, but if you are willing to do that, you could make a very secure investment in a different geographical location.

You can also look at the type of properties that you are investing in and do something a little different. For example, if all of your property investments are long-term real estate investments, you can have a look at short-term rentals as an option. Different real estate investments will help you diversify your portfolio. You may also want to try a different investment strategy, such as house flipping or holding your investments for a longer time so they increase in value. Perhaps moving to a more active or passive investment is something that could also appeal to you, depending on your goals and what you have experienced in the past.

When you reinvest the money you have made through one of your investments, you are taking advantage of compounding your profits. You are essentially accelerating the growth of your wealth over time to increase it at an exponential rate. The more money you put into your investments, the more money you could potentially get out of it. This is why it is so important to think continuously about how to invest and get more out of your investments. The goal is to take advantage of the investment market so you can maximize your profits and ensure you are seeing the best returns possible.

WHY INFLATION IS AN ALLY

Whenever the topic of inflation is brought up, it typically has a negative connotation to it. This is understandable because when the price of things increases, your general profit may decrease since you are paying more money for the upkeep of your property. However, inflation can work to your benefit. When inflation hits, it means that the general prices of things increase, which also means that rent increases and the amount people will spend on properties will also increase. Essentially, you can charge a lot more rent or sell your property for more when experiencing higher inflation. This works best if you purchased your investment property when inflation was lower and the general price of things was also lower.

You can use inflation to your advantage when it comes to your real estate investment. One way is to focus on properties that generate a steady cash flow. When your real estate investments generate high cash flow, you can make more money when interest increases. If the prices of everything are already increasing, it means that you will probably be able to charge more rent on your properties and make more money. In this case, it might also be a good idea to go for short-term leases rather than longer-term ones. If you know that inflation will be a risk soon, you may want to lock in shorter-term leases so that you can increase the rent prices should inflation occur. If you and your tenant have a long-term lease, that means that you have to accept their rental payments at a fixed rate until the lease is terminated. A shorter-term lease means you can change the agreed-upon rental price based on factors such as inflation.

Diversifying your investment portfolio is a good way to protect yourself from interest rates. Diversification is incredibly important. You are investing, which means you are spreading out your investments and effectively lowering the risk you are facing. Where one investment may have a negative outlook when it comes to inflation, another investment might give you positive benefits when faced with inflation.

A huge part of being an investor is being knowledgeable about what is going on in the economy and the general market. While you can never fully predict what will happen with the economy, monitoring economic indicators is still a good idea. This way, you can prepare for any changes in the state of the economy. This may mean that you need to make different investments, sell your investments, or invest more heavily in what you currently are investing in. There will always be trends in the market, and staying aware and up-to-date with these will allow you to make better investment decisions. You can try to follow professionals on various social media platforms, newsletters, magazines, and other types of content. This will keep you in the loop with what is happening and help you be constantly notified when things are changing so you know what to expect. It is always better to be prepared rather than to be caught off guard.

INTERACTIVE ELEMENT: REFLECTION QUESTIONS

It is always important to reflect when it comes to your investment decisions. As you move through life, your investment choices will look different based on various factors. The goals you set five years ago might not be relevant now, and you will need to shift your goals and thought patterns to move into something better for the future. As you gain more experience in real estate investing, you may realize that your investment style changes, and so do the things you need and want. Ask the reflection questions below every once in a while so you can see where you stand when it comes to your investments:

- What are your long-term and short-term goals regarding your finances and real estate investing?
- How will you use real estate to help you reach your financial and personal goals?
- In which ways do you plan to diversify your investment portfolio?
- What strategy are you going to use to reinvest your profits from your current investments into future investments so you can build long-term wealth?

With a comprehensive understanding of long-term success strategies in real estate, you're now equipped to navigate the market confidently and build substantial wealth.

INSPIRE NEW INVESTORS TO GET STARTED!

You're about to begin one of the most exciting and rewarding ventures you've ever committed to—and this is your chance to inspire others and let them in on how to break into real estate investment.

Simply by sharing your honest opinion of this book and a little about your own story, you'll inspire new readers to take the plunge —and you'll show them exactly where they can find all the information they need to make a success of it.

LEAVE A REVIEW!

Thank you so much for your support. I wish you every success with your investments!

Scan the QR code below

CONCLUSION

Investing in real estate is one of the most rewarding journeys you can go on. It definitely takes a lot of work, but all the effort you will put in will be worth it. When you invest in real estate, you are also investing in your future. There is a reason so many people want to get into real estate. Now that you have reached the end of this book, you have all the tools you need to become a successful real estate investor. Just remember that all it takes is one small step at a time. You don't have to put pressure on yourself to become a multimillionaire in a matter of months. Taking a few small steps at a time is the best way to approach investing in real estate. Focus on one aspect first and then keep building on that momentum.

There are so many types of real estate out there that you can find one that suits your needs and financial goals. If you are a beginner investor and don't have a lot of funds to play with, then you can start small by investing in a real estate investment trust. This is a great place to start, so you can get a feel for investing in real estate without actually purchasing a property. From there, you can continuously build up and then take steps toward other types of real estate investments. As long as you have a plan and are taking action to stick to it, then you are on the right path. There is no one way to be a real estate investor, so it is up to you to create a strategy and a plan that is going to work for you and your finances. The power is completely in your hands, and you can tailor your investment strategy while using the principles in this book to help guide you.

You've learned the essentials of real estate investing, from financing and purchasing properties to managing short-term rentals and leveraging long-term strategies. Now, it's time to put these insights into action and start building your real estate empire!

If you have found this book helpful, I'd really appreciate it if you gave it a positive review on the platform where you purchased it. This will help to extend my reach and ensure more people are well-equipped for the fulfilling journey of investing in real estate. Don't forget to check out my other books as well!

ALSO BY FRANK EBERSTADT

How to launch your own Airbnb empire from scratch — no property management experience required.

Data from Stratos Jet Charters show that **approximately 14,000 new hosts are joining Airbnb... *every month.***

So if you plan on turning a decent profit with your Airbnb listing, you will have to find creative ways to stand out from the competition.

The good news is there's nothing to worry about.

Because the truth is anyone can start their own Airbnb rental business.

All you need are **practical strategies and principles that have been proven to work repeatedly.**

In this book, you'll discover:

- The simple **6-step framework for launching an Airbnb listing from scratch**
- The 4 primary types of Airbnb accommodations and which one you should use for your property

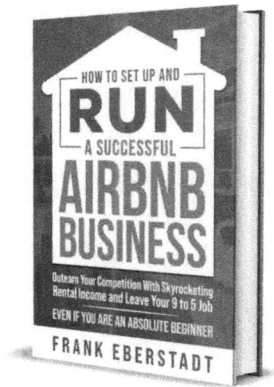

- How to calculate the profitability of your Airbnb listing — always look at these 5 factors
- **Airbnb Insurance: what's included and what additional coverage you might need**
- The 7 best safety tips for Airbnb hosts
- **The subtle difference between a house manual and house rules**
- **3 core components of any effective Airbnb listing — focus on THIS element above all others**
- How to automate these behind-the-scenes processes for your Airbnb business
- **9 signs that starting your own short-term rental business is the perfect fit for you**

And much more!

There's no secret "hack" to winning on Airbnb.

And unlike other guides that promote overly complex strategies filled with technical terminology… this book is designed specifically for *anyone* to understand.

So whether you're already an Airbnb host or have just discovered how Airbnb works, you'll have all the fundamental knowledge you need to start earning rental income on the side.

Scan the QR code below and get your copy now.

Unlock the secrets to skyrocketing your rental income and bookings with this comprehensive guide to mastering Airbnb!

Your Airbnb property isn't just bricks and mortar—it's a treasure chest of untapped potential. If you only had the right map to guide you, imagine the possibilities.

You could unlock your property's full potential, transform your Airbnb business into a consistent income generator, and finally leave behind the days of just scraping by.

This is where Frank Eberstadt steps in.

He's back with his latest book that promises to be the companion that steers you beyond Airbnb basics and puts you confidently in the driver's seat.

Inside, you will discover:

- **How to research your market effectively and outsmart your competition** – identify your unique selling proposition and elevate your Airbnb above the competition!
- **An arsenal of advanced pricing strategies tailored for different seasons and property types** – navigate the tumultuous tides of seasonal demands and make sure your rental rates are always on point
- **The magic of transitioning and diversification to ensure consistent income** – you no longer need to worry about slow seasons

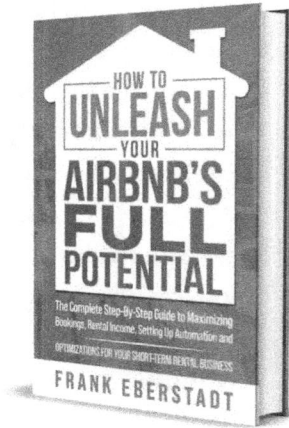

- **The power of data analytics and metrics to make informed business decisions** – drive informed decisions to boost your income
- **Tips and tricks to optimize your Airbnb listing and attract more bookings** – make your listing so appealing that guests can't resist clicking "book now"!
- **Secrets to building a stellar reputation and becoming a beloved Superhost** – charm your guests and earn glowing 5-star reviews with ease!
- **Techniques to automate your Airbnb business and save valuable time** – imagine spending less time on admin and more time enjoying the fruits of your success

And much more!

Wave goodbye to frustration and uncertainty – step into a future where your Airbnb investment transforms into a consistent income-generating machine!

It is time to up your Airbnb game.

Scan the QR code below and get your copy now.

GLOSSARY

1031 Exchange: This allows for tax to be deferred by selling a property and using that money to buy a new property without paying capital gains tax on the sale.

Amortization: An accounting method to spread loan payments over a certain time. The payments will cover the principal and interest.

ARM: Also known as adjustable-rate mortgage. With this type of loan, the interest rate adjusts or changes over time.

Amenity: This refers to an extra feature or appliance that a property has.

Appreciation: When the value of a property increases over time due to market demand, improvements, or inflation.

APR (Annual Percentage Rate): The yearly cost of a loan, including all additional fees and rates.

BRRRR: This refers to an investment strategy where you buy, rehab, rent, refinance, and repeat.

Cash Flow: The net amount being transferred in and out of an investment after income and expenses.

Cap Rate (Capitalization Rate): This is used to assess how profitable a real estate investment will be by dividing the NOI by the purchase price.

CMA: A comparative market analysis, which is a report on the market value of a property based on a comparison of similar properties in the same area.

Collateral: Pledging an asset for a loan so if you default on the loan, the lender can repossess it to get their money out.

Depreciation: The value of an asset decreases over time due to various factors.

Equity: The difference between the market value and the amount owed on the property.

Fair Market Value: The estimated price a property can be sold for on the current market.

HELOC: Also known as Home Equity Line of Credit, it allows a borrower to take out credit up to a certain limit by leveraging equity in a property they currently own.

Homeowners Association (HOA): An organization that manages the affairs and operations of a certain group of properties that are owned or rented by multiple different people.

HVAC: Heating, Ventilation, and Air Conditioning system.

Interest Rate: A percentage fee that is charged on a loan.

Leverage: To use a loan or credit to purchase a piece of real estate.

Liquidity: Signifies how quickly an asset can be sold or converted into cash.

LMI (Lenders Mortgage Insurance): Insurance that protects the lender if the borrower defaults on a loan.

LTV: This stands for loan-to-value ratio and is used to calculate the potential risk of a loan compared to the value of the property.

NOI: This stands for net operating income and indicates the income generated after subtracting the expenses.

Principal: The original amount of money borrowed, without the additional fees or interest.

REIT: Also known as a Real Estate Investment Trust. This entity pools together investment capital from multiple investors to purchase, operate, or finance properties to generate investment returns.

ROI (Return on Investment): Evaluates the profitability of an investment. This is calculated by dividing the net profit by the investment cost.

REFERENCES

"3 Highly Motivational Real Estate Success Stories - New Silver," January 25, 2024. https://newsilver.com/the-lender/real-estate-success-stories/.

"7 Pros and Cons of Owning a Short Term Rental | Short Term Rental Manager," April 20, 2018. https://shorttermrentalmanager.com/7-pros-and-cons-of-owning-a-short-term-rental/.

"10 Common Rental Property Repairs Landlords Need to Know About | Travelers Insurance," November 14, 2022. https://www.travelers.com/resources/home/landlords/10-common-rental-property-repairs-landlords-need-to-know-about.

"20 Expert Tips for Successfully Managing an Airbnb Remotely." https://awning.com/post/manage-airbnb-remotely.

"50 Questions To Ask Before Investing in Real Estate." https://www.linkedin.com/pulse/50-questions-ask-before-investing-real-estate-camaplan.

Admin. "Land Investing - How To Make Money in 9 Steps." *Best Real Estate Investment Company in Lekki, Lagos, Nigeria* (blog), May 16, 2022. https://eystone.ng/land-investing/.

Guest Author. "How and Why You Need to Diversify Your Real Estate Portfolio - Stessa." https://www.stessa.com/blog/how-and-why-you-need-to-diversify-your-real-estate-portfolio/.

Booking Ninjas. "What Is a Residential Property? Types, Features, and Benefits." https://www.bookingninjas.com/blog/what-is-a-residential-property-types-features-and-benefits.

Brown, Jerry. "27 Loan Terminologies You Must Know." Forbes Advisor, February 9, 2021. https://www.forbes.com/advisor/personal-loans/loan-terminologies/.

Cain, Sarah Li. "10 Key Questions To Ask When Buying A House." Bankrate, July 17, 2024. https://www.bankrate.com/real-estate/questions-to-ask-when-buying-a-house/.

Contributor, Guest. "8 Strategies for Real Estate Investing During Inflation." REtipster, August 3, 2023. https://retipster.com/8-strategies-for-real-estate-investing-during-inflation/.

DeAngelo, Nic. "Understanding Compounding in Real Estate." *Saint Investment* (blog), September 28, 2023. https://saintinvestment.com/blog/understanding-compounding-in-real-estate/.

Dieker, Nicole. "Why Is Good Credit So Important?" Bankrate, November 3, 2023. https://www.bankrate.com/credit-cards/advice/why-is-good-credit-so-important/.

Drake Law. "Key Legal Factors to Consider Before Investing in Real Estate." https://www.drakelaw.ca/legal-insights/key-legal-factors-to-consider-before-investing-in-real-estate.

Elphick, Dean. "Airbnb Superhost: How to Become a Superhost on Airbnb." Little Hotelier, October 10, 2022. https://www.littlehotelier.com/blog/get-more-bookings/airbnb-superhost/.

Ferran. "10 Ways To Make More Money From Rental Properties." *June Homes Blog* (blog), January 23, 2024. https://junehomes.com/blog/2024/01/23/make-more-money-from-rental-properties/.

Fettke, Kathy. "Top 60 Real Estate Definitions for Investors to Know." *RealWealth* (blog). https://realwealth.com/learn/real-estate-definitions/.

FortuneBuilders. "House Hacking: A Beginner's Guide," September 21, 2022. https://www.fortunebuilders.com/p/what-is-house-hacking/.

Griggs Homes. "What Is Property Development and How Does It Work?" https://www.griggshomes.co.uk/what-is-property-development-how-does-it-work.

Hamed, Eman. "The Complete Beginner's Guide to Investing in Long-Term Rentals." *Learn Real Estate Investing | Mashvisor Real Estate Blog* (blog), March 7, 2019. https://www.mashvisor.com/blog/beginners-guide-long-term-rentals/.

Harrington, Dennis. "The Rise of Renters by Choice." Multifamily Executive, May 18, 2022. https://www.multifamilyexecutive.com/property-management/demographics/the-rise-of-renters-by-choice_o.

"Highlights From the Profile of Home Buyers and Sellers," November 13, 2023. https://www.nar.realtor/research-and-statistics/research-reports/highlights-from-the-profile-of-home-buyers-and-sellers.

"How Much Should I Charge for Rent: Tips to Rental Rates." https://www.mysmartmove.com/blog/how-much-charge-for-rent.

https://prenohq.com/. "How to Start an Airbnb: A Beginners Guide." https://prenohq.com/blog/how-to-list-your-property-on-airbnb/.

Investopedia. "5 Negotiating Strategies When Selling Your Home." https://www.investopedia.com/articles/mortgages-real-estate/12/playing-hardball-when-selling-your-home.asp.

Investopedia. "Calculating Net Operating Income (NOI) for Real Estate." https://www.investopedia.com/terms/n/noi.asp.

Investopedia. "Capitalization Rate: Cap Rate Defined With Formula and Examples." https://www.investopedia.com/terms/c/capitalizationrate.asp.

Investopedia. "Commercial Real Estate: Definition and Types." https://www.investopedia.com/terms/c/commercialrealestate.asp.

Investopedia. "Fixed-Rate Mortgage: How It Works, Types, vs. Adjustable Rate." https://www.investopedia.com/terms/f/fixed-rate_mortgage.asp.

Investopedia. "How Airbnb Works—for Hosts, Guests, and the Company Itself." https://www.investopedia.com/articles/personal-finance/032814/pros-and-cons-using-airbnb.asp.

Investopedia. "How to Profit From Inflation." https://www.investopedia.com/articles/investing/080813/how-profit-inflation.asp.

Investopedia. "Interest-Only Mortgage: Definition, How They Work, Pros and Cons." https://www.investopedia.com/terms/i/interestonlymortgage.asp.

Investopedia. "Loan Terms: Specific Terms Defined and How to Negotiate Them." https://www.investopedia.com/loan-terms-5075341.

Investopedia. "REIT: What It Is and How To Invest." https://www.investopedia.com/terms/r/reit.asp.

Investopedia. "Rent-to-Own Homes: How the Process Works." https://www.investopedia.com/updates/rent-to-own-homes/.

Investopedia. "Residential Rental Property Definition, Tax Pros & Cons." https://www.investopedia.com/terms/r/residentialrentalproperty.asp.

Investopedia. "What Is a 1031 Exchange? Know the Rules." https://www.investopedia.com/financial-edge/0110/10-things-to-know-about-1031-exchanges.aspx.

Investopedia. "What Is Comparative Market Analysis (CMA) in Real Estate?" https://www.investopedia.com/terms/c/comparative-market-analysis.asp.

Investopedia. "What You Should Know About Real Estate Valuation." https://www.investopedia.com/articles/realestate/12/real-estate-valuation.asp.

"Key Financial Metrics for Real Estate Investors | Cg Tax, Audit & Advisory," October 24, 2023. https://www.cgteam.com/key-financial-metrics-for-real-estate-investors/.

Landon, Dena. "The Top 10 Metrics Every Real Estate Investor Should Know (and Why) - Stessa." https://www.stessa.com/blog/10-real-estate-investing-metrics/.

Lodgify. "All About Short-Term Rentals," n.d. https://www.lodgify.com/guides/business/short-term/.

Lodgify. "What Is a Vacation Rental?" n.d. https://www.lodgify.com/encyclopedia/vacation-rental/.

Mann (Silvermann), Baruch. "How Does Inflation Affect Real Estate? Here's What You Need to Know." Entrepreneur, December 2, 2022. https://www.entrepreneur.com/money-finance/how-does-inflation-affect-real-estate-heres-what-you-need/433953.

Marketing. "Giving Rehab Property a Makeover: A Real Estate Investor's Guide." Reedy & Company, December 7, 2023. https://www.reedyandcompany.com/blog/giving-rehab-property-a-makeover-a-real-estate-investors-guide/.

Martin, Allison. "Cash-Out Refinancing: What It Is, How It Works." Bankrate, September 5, 2024. https://www.bankrate.com/mortgages/cash-out-refinancing/.

McCracken, Madison. "The Importance of Thorough Tenant Screening Process." *Bay Property Management Group* (blog), April 6, 2022. https://www.baymgmtgroup.com/blog/tenant-screening/.

Memphis Investment Properties. "7 Benefits of Owning a Rental Property," November 8, 2021. https://www.memphisinvestmentproperties.net/7-benefits-of-owning-a-rental-property/.

NerdWallet. "How to Buy a House: 15 Steps in the Homebuying Process," March 19, 2024. https://www.nerdwallet.com/article/mortgages/home-buying-checklist-steps-to-buying-house.

NerdWallet. "How to Get Preapproved for a Mortgage," April 25, 2024. https://www.nerdwallet.com/article/mortgages/how-to-get-a-mortgage-preapproval.

New Western. "Marketing Your Investment: Step-by-Step Guide on Selling Your Investment Property Like the Pros." https://www.newwestern.com/guide/selling-a-rental-property/.

Newsroom. "Airbnb Q4-2023 and Full-Year Financial Results." Airbnb, February 13, 2024. https://news.airbnb.com/airbnb-q4-2023-and-full-year-financial-results/.

Oak, Red. "Top 7 Reasons Why 90% of US Millionaires Invest In Real Estate & Why You Should Follow the Lead." *Red Oak Development Group* (blog), August 3, 2022. https://redoakvc.com/top-7-reasons-why-90-of-us-millionaires-invest-in-real-estate-why-you-should-follow-the-lead/.

Ostrowski, Jeff. "What Is A HELOC (Home Equity Line Of Credit)?" Bankrate, April 24, 2024. https://www.bankrate.com/home-equity/what-is-heloc/.

Passive Real Estate Investing. "From Zero to 35 Rentals in 4 Years – A Client Success Story," January 30, 2018. https://www.passiverealestateinvesting.com/from-zero-to-35-rentals-in-4-years-a-client-success-story/.

Rajkhar. "Tax Saving by Investing in Real Estate." Reddit, 2024. https://www.reddit.com/r/realestateinvesting/comments/1blsscr/tax_saving_by_investing_in_real_estate/.

"Real Estate Risks: What It Is and How to Avoid Them." https://www.mandanibay.com/blog/risks-of-real-estate-investment-and-how-to-avoid-them/.

Richards, Laurie. "What Is A Balloon Mortgage And Why Is It Risky?" Bankrate, July 15, 2024. https://www.bankrate.com/mortgages/what-is-a-balloon-mortgage/.

Rocket Mortgage. "Lease Option: Definition And How It Works." https://www.rocketmortgage.com/learn/lease-option.

Rocket Mortgage. "Seller Financing: How It Works, Pros And Cons And If It's A Good Idea." https://www.rocketmortgage.com/learn/seller-financing.

Rocket Mortgage. "Top 6 Tax Benefits Of Real Estate Investing." https://www.rock etmortgage.com/learn/tax-benefits-of-real-estate-investing.

Rocket Mortgage. "Understanding The BRRRR Method Of Real Estate Investment." https://www.rocketmortgage.com/learn/brrrr.

Rodriguez, Amanda. "Understanding NOI/Cap Rate & How to Calculate Them." *Learn Real Estate Investing | Mashvisor Real Estate Blog* (blog), July 10, 2023. https://www.mashvisor.com/blog/noi-cap-rate/.

Rohde, Jeff. "What Is Due Diligence in Real Estate? A Simple Guide and Checklist." https://learn.roofstock.com/blog/what-is-due-diligence-in-real-estate.

Samurai, Financial. "When To Sell An Investment Property: Every Indicator To Consider." *Financial Samurai* (blog), August 17, 2019. https://www.financial samurai.com/when-to-sell-an-investment-property/.

"Self-Management vs. Property Company: Which Is Better? | BiggerPockets Blog," May 12, 2023. https://www.biggerpockets.com/blog/property-management-vs-self-management.

Sharkey, Sarah. "Putting A Down Payment On Investment Property: What To Know." Quicken Loans, October 20, 2023. https://www.quickenloans.com/learn/down-payment-on-investment-property.

Strategies for Influence. 2019. "Robert Kiyosaki - Rich Dad Poor Dad." Strategies for Influence. November 17, 2019. https://strategiesforinfluence.com/robert-kiyosaki-rich-dad-poor-dad/.

"Successfully Estimating Renovation Costs in Real Estate." https://www.dealma chine.com/blog/successfully-estimating-renovation-costs-in-real-estate.

Team, BnB Hosts. "How to Handle The Most Common Airbnb Guest Enquiries Like a Pro." *BnB Hosts* (blog), September 24, 2019. https://www.bnbhosts.com. au/common-airbnb-enquiries/.

"The 7 Best Short Term Rental Sites | Uplisting.Io." https://www.uplisting.io/blog/the-7-best-short-term-rental-sites-for-hosts.

The Balance. "How You Can Build (or Lose) Equity in Your Home." https://www. thebalancemoney.com/definition-of-equity-1798546.

"The Ultimate 35-Point House Rehab Checklist." https://www.theinvestorsedge. com/blog/the-ultimate-36-point-house-rehab-checklist.

"The Ultimate Airbnb Maintenance Checklist and Schedule | Minut." https://www. minut.com/blog/airbnb-maintenance-checklist-and-schedule.

Todd, Jonny. "Viewing a House Checklist: Key Questions to Ask When Buying." Ellis & Co, July 26, 2022. https://www.ellisandco.co.uk/guides/buying/view ing-a-house-checklist-8457/.

Tom. "How to Get Your Airbnb Pricing Strategies Right: 7 Steps." *Host Tools* (blog), July 24, 2020. https://hosttools.com/blog/short-term-rental-tips/airbnb-pricing-strategies/.

Tross, Kasey. "The 6 Types of Commercial Real Estate Property." *VTS* (blog), May 8, 2023. https://www.vts.com/blog/the-6-types-of-commercial-real-estate-properties.

TRVLGUIDES [Learn How To Travel]. "How To Create An Airbnb Account [Or Change Or Delete It]." https://trvlguides.com/articles/create-airbnb-account.

Ugazu, Yassine. "Glossary of Real Estate & Vacation Rental Investing Terms." *Learn Real Estate Investing | Mashvisor Real Estate Blog* (blog), August 24, 2023. https://www.mashvisor.com/blog/real-estate-investing-terms/.

Wall Street Prep. "Net Operating Income (NOI) | Formula + Calculator." https://www.wallstreetprep.com/knowledge/noi-net-operating-income/.

"What Is a Variable Rate Mortgage and How Do They Work | L&C." https://www.landc.co.uk/mortgage-guides/variable-rate-mortgage.

"What Is the Due Diligence Period in Real Estate? - Experian," November 4, 2022. https://www.experian.com/blogs/ask-experian/what-is-due-diligence-period-real-estate/.

"What Is Real Estate Appreciation?" https://smartasset.com/investing/real-estate-appreciation.

"What Is Underwriting In Real Estate? Full Guide." https://www.metawealth.co/post/what-is-underwriting-in-real-estate-explained.

"What's a REIT (Real Estate Investment Trust)?" https://www.reit.com/what-reit.

Wieland, David. "Council Post: Assessing Three Types Of Risk In Real Estate." Forbes. https://www.forbes.com/councils/forbesrealestatecouncil/2020/08/05/assessing-three-types-of-risk-in-real-estate/.

Yale, Laura Grace Tarpley, CEPF, Aly J. "Saving for a Down Payment: Strategies to Achieve Homeownership." Business Insider. https://www.businessinsider.com/personal-finance/mortgages/tips-for-saving-for-a-down-payment.

"Your Essential Guide to Navigating Real Estate & Your Credit," July 27, 2023. https://mathesonattys.com/blog/real-estate-and-your-credit/.

Yuhenyo. "Property Is Severely Under Valued by Potential Lender Bank." Reddit, 2023. https://www.reddit.com/r/AusPropertyChat/comments/180asha/property_is_severely_under_valued_by_potential/.

Zillow. "75% of Recent Home Buyers Have Regrets about Their New Home." https://www.prnewswire.com/news-releases/75-of-recent-home-buyers-have-regrets-about-their-new-home-301477283.html.

Zinn, Dori. "Flipping Houses: A How-To Guide For Beginners." Bankrate, July 8, 2024. https://www.bankrate.com/real-estate/flipping-houses/.

IMAGE REFERENCES

BP, Steve. *Calculator, Calculation, Insurance Image.* July 9, 2014. Photograph. https://pixabay.com/photos/calculator-calculation-insurance-385506/.

Kuhar, Milivoj. *Man Climbing on Ladder Inside Room.* February 2, 2018. Image. https://unsplash.com/photos/man-climbing-on-ladder-inside-room-Te48TPzdcU8.

Li, Kostiantyn. *A House Made out of Money on a White Background.* October 20, 2021. Image. https://unsplash.com/photos/a-house-made-out-of-money-on-a-white-background-1sCXwVoqKAw.

Mallorca, Tierra. *White and Red Wooden House Miniature on Brown Table.* June 14, 2019. Photograph. https://unsplash.com/photos/white-and-red-wooden-house-miniature-on-brown-table-rgJ1J8SDEAY.

Tingey Injury Law Firm. *A Wooden Gavel on a White Marble Backdrop.* May 13, 2020. Photograph. https://unsplash.com/photos/brown-wooden-smoking-pipe-on-white-surface-6sl88x150Xs.

Wheeler, Blake. *Housing Development American Fork.* April 4, 2017. Photograph. https://unsplash.com/photos/aerial-photography-houses-zBHU08hdzhY.

ABOUT THE AUTHOR

Frank Eberstadt is an accommodation manager and the bestselling author of *How to Set Up and Run a Successful Airbnb Business* & *How to Unleash Your Airbnb's Full Potential*.

His books address property management and business growth in Airbnb, guiding readers to seek and capitalize on opportunities in the market, nurturing successful businesses on the way.

Frank is the accommodation manager for an investment group operating hotels and motels in Australia. He has established his own successful Airbnb business, and has grown his portfolio to six properties. Frank began his first Airbnb business from the ground up and knows how hard it can be to break into property listings and attract guests. Using his extensive experience in the accommodation industry, his aim is to lay out a clear, step-by-step path that even complete newbies can follow to success.

Frank's interest in vacation property stems from his many years traveling as a solo backpacker, something he now does with his family. These two very different traveling experiences have fed into his awareness of what makes a successful vacation rental, and have been key to his success as an Airbnb business owner.

Frank still loves to travel, and enjoys surfing, but more than anything, he loves to spend quality time with his family, no matter where their adventures take them.

www.ingramcontent.com/pod-product-compliance
Lightning Source LLC
Chambersburg PA
CBHW030518210326
41597CB00013B/953